Involving Parents
in their Children's Learning

Involving Parents in their Children's Learning

Margy Whalley

and the Pen Green Centre Team

P·C·P
Paul Chapman
Publishing Ltd

Paul Chapman Publishing Ltd
A SAGE Publications Company
6 Bonhill Street
London EC2A 4PU

SAGE Publications Inc.
2455 Teller Road
Thousand Oaks, California 91320

SAGE Publications India Pvt Ltd
32, M-Block Market
Greater Kailash-I
New Delhi 110 048

British Cataloguing in Publication Data

A catalogue record for this book is available from the
British Library

ISBN 0 7619 7071 1
ISBN 0 7619 7072 X (pbk)

Library of Congress catalog card number is available

Typeset by Anneset, Weston-super-Mare, Somerset
Printed and bound in Great Britain by Athenaeum Press,
Gateshead

Contents

Notes on the Team

Cath Arnold is Head of Nursery at the Pen Green Centre for Under Fives and their families. She has over 20 years' experience in both private and public sector childcare and education. She is a qualified teacher, has a Master's Degree in Education and has recently had her first book published. She is a parent and grandparent.

Trevor Chandler trained as a social worker. He has worked at Pen Green for 14 years, originally as Deputy Head and subsequently as Head of Centre. He has just completed an MA in Education with Care. Trevor has two children, Rachel and David.

Annette Cummings is a teacher/senior family worker in the nursery and the parent of two children. She originally became involved with the work of the Pen Green Centre as a parent and returned to university in 1996/97 to gain a PGCE.

Marcus Dennison was a family worker at Pen Green for seven years and is now working in the care sector. He runs groups at Pen Green for parents during the day and in the evening.

Colette Tait is a research assistant at the Pen Green Research Base. She has two children, Georgia and Harry, who both attended Pen Green nursery. Colette ran groups at Pen Green as a parent volunteer and subsequently took up an administrative post. She is currently undertaking an MA in Psychoanalytic Observational Studies at the Tavistock Institute.

Margy Whalley has a 20-year-old daughter and has worked for over 27 years in education and care settings in Britain, Brazil and Papua New Guinea. She is a qualified teacher with an MA in Community Education and a Doctorate in leadership within early years settings. She is currently directing the research programme at the Pen Green Research Base, and is involved in the Early Excellence Centre evaluation and research and evaluation work for Corby Sure Start.

To my daughter Natasha, now aged 20 and very much a
'shining light powerful beyond measure'

Acknowledgements

We would like to acknowledge our huge debt to Chris Athey, who directed the Froebel Early Education Project 1973–78 and Professor Tina Bruce, who worked alongside her. They were the pioneers and they have inspired and supported us.

We also want to acknowledge Professor Ferre Laevers, Professor Chris Pascal and Dr Tony Bertram, and thank them for sharing their work with us.

Finally, we need to thank the Esmee Fairbairn Charitable Trust who funded this project, our Advisory Group, who supported and sustained us over five years, and the staff, parents and children at Pen Green, who became so deeply involved.

Preface

This book is just one of the outcomes of a five-year research and development project at the Pen Green Centre for under 5s and their families. In it we describe the rich and challenging dialogue that can develop when early years practitioners, supported by colleagues in institutions of higher education, work collaboratively with children and families.

Small-scale innovative projects such as this one, with its focus on involving parents, have a major contribution to make, not just to the community which they serve but also to the wider early years community (Oliver, Smith and Barker, 1998). Practitioner research can inform the wider debate about the ethical dimension of research and can demonstrate how much more effective it is to work in a genuine research partnership with those who have traditionally been the objects of research (Pascal, 1996).

This research project was set up in 1995. It was part funded during 1996 by the Teacher Training Agency and subsequently was fully funded from 1997 to 2000 by the Esmee Fairbairn Charitable Trust; we are very grateful to our funders for giving us the opportunity to work so closely and thoughtfully with parents and children. The full research report is available from the Pen Green Research, Training and Development Base. A VHS video illustrating much of this project has also been produced with support from the Department for Education and Employment (DfEE). This video will be distributed as part of a training programme delivered by staff and parents at the Pen Green Centre.

Early years educators rarely have enough non-contact time to develop their skills as reflective practitioners. Our vision for the future is that there will be many early years centres across the public, private and voluntary sector where staff can develop innovative projects with the same kind of support:

Imagine early years centres where all staff are beginning to be assertive; self critical and supportively critical of other, where the staff are deeply attached to each other, work cooperatively, respect each other's strengths, and celebrate each other's successes and failures. Centres in which the adults, parents and staff are rigorous thinkers, focused and analytical, and yet aware of the rhythms of the organisation and their personal lives; where the work is rooted in the local community but staff also reach out, make their views known and challenge local and central Government over important issues. These would be centres in which children's rich emotional lives were acknowledged and supported, where children were encouraged and cognitively challenged and their learning was promoted. In such centres children could truly become the managers of their own possibilities.

(Adapted from Whalley, 1999a, p. 336)

1

New Forms of Provision, New Ways of Working – the Pen Green Centre

Margy Whalley

The Pen Green Centre for under 5s and their families opened in 1983. It was set up as a multifunctional service for children and families and was staffed by a multidisciplinary team.

The centre was financed by Northamptonshire County Council and was jointly managed by the Education and Social Services Departments and the local health authority. In 1983 Pen Green had six staff and worked with 50 children; today the centre has more than 35 staff, including teachers, social workers, nursery nurses and support staff, and we work with over 500 families.

Corby, where the centre is based, was a steel town in the 1930s with a teeming population of steelworkers who had come down from Scotland and across from Central Europe to find work. By the 1980s, when the Pen Green Centre opened, the steelworks had closed, the housing estates were boarded up, shops were barricaded with wire grills and 43 per cent of the male population was unemployed. Poor nutrition, inadequate housing and high infant mortality rates were all major factors influencing the lives of young families. There were minimal statutory services for parents and young children and very few of the traditional voluntary services for families in need of support.

In Corby in the early 1980s, as in some parts of the UK today, there was no choice of services for parents wanting nursery education, childcare or 'time out' to study. There was no partnership between the public, private and voluntary sectors because there was so little provision. There was only one private day nursery, a small number of registered childminders and a few playgroups. The part-time nursery education that was provided in nursery units attached to primary schools was hugely oversubscribed, and these nursery sessions did not help parents who wanted to attend college or go back to work.

1

There was also a social services children's centre in Corby which was perceived by local parents as a resource exclusively for 'problem families'.

The Pen Green Centre was set up in what was formerly a comprehensive school built in the 1930s to provide an education for the children of the steelworkers. The houses that surround the centre were once steelworkers' homes. Sixty feet away stood the last of the blast furnaces which had transformed a small Northamptonshire village into a steel town (Whalley, 1994).

Problems and contradictions

Corby in the 1980s exemplified many of the problems and contradictions inherent in education and daycare services in the UK at this time. These were some of the issues which staff at Pen Green had to face:

1 *Simplistic demarcation lines:* crude divisions remained between those that saw themselves as providers for the educational needs of the child (the local education authority – LEA) and those supporting the child in terms of welfare and childcare (Social Services, the private sector).

2 *Separatism:* in that there was no tradition of working in an integrated way with other agencies such as health and the Adult Education Services, both of which have a critical role in working with children and their families.

3 *Over-professionalism:* This meant that the contribution of the voluntary sector had been underestimated and the energy and commitment of the local community was largely unrecognized.

4 *Monoculturalism:* when setting up early childhood services there had been no attempt to learn from other European countries such as Scandinavia or Italy where integrated services for young children have a long history.

5 *Europhobia:* in that the only 'models' generally recognized as successful in the 1980s were those that had been transplanted from the USA. There was very little recognition of the importance of a local diagnosis of need.

6 *Compensatory models:* because professionals who worked with parents were still assuming a 'deficit' model of parenting which was based on the premise that some parents are ineffective and that they can become more effective by being taught a set of 'parenting skills'.

7 *Political will:* since most early years educators did not recognize the

political nature of early years work and had little experience of engaging in political debate.

8 *Lack of accountability*: this was manifested as a general lack of awareness of the changing needs of families, and the need for flexible and responsive services. There had also been a failure locally to recognize the issues of the stakeholders – children, parents, families and the wider community.

9 *Poor conditions of service and training*: although early childhood educators were powerful advocates for children and families they were traditionally fairly passive in relation to their own conditions of service. Staff were accustomed to working long hours with poor pay, inadequate training and little if any non-contact time to be able to plan and reflect on children's learning.

Working with the community

Pen Green as a centre for children and families developed from a perspective, 'which regards early childhood services as a need and right for all communities and families, and as an expression of social solidarity with children and parents' (Moss, 1992, p. 43). However, this social solidarity was born in the first instance out of conflict.

When the centre was set up staff had to work with a very vocal and often hostile group of people, since the strongest voluntary group in the local community was a parents' action group *against* the centre. This group comprised local residents who felt that there had not been enough consultation between those setting up the new early years service and those who were expected to use it. They were afraid that the local authority planned to set up a daycare service for vulnerable families and this was not what they wanted. They were clear that what was needed in their community was a radically new kind of service.

The visions and principles behind the services that were set up at Pen Green were carved out by this 'local action group', local politicians, local authority officers and the newly appointed staff group. Their big idea, their vision for the future, was that in this small community there should be a service for children aged under 5 and their families, a service which would honour the needs of young children and celebrate their existence. It would also support families, however they were constituted within the community.

This vision was underpinned by the belief that:

- the most effective way of delivering coherent education, health and social services to young families was through an integrated centre which would be easily accessible (i.e., at pram-pushing distance); ·

- services should be flexible and responsive to the needs of all local children and their extended families;
- education and care are indivisible, that the early years curriculum offered in these services should be developmentally appropriate for children from 0 to 5 years and should recognize the central position of play in early learning;
- services should respect and value children and parents' individual differences and celebrate ethnic, linguistic and cultural diversity;
- education begins at birth – services must recognize the key role parents play as their child's first educators, and parents' commitment to their children's early education;
- parent education and adult community education should be made available to parents *within* services for early childhood education and care;
- all the staff working in these settings need to be highly trained, reflective practitioners with equitable conditions of service (i.e., adequate pay, non-contact time, in-service training, supervision, opportunities for promotion, etc); and
- workers in early childhood settings need to be concerned with power sharing and community regeneration.

Principles

The staff group appointed to work at Pen Green in the early 1980s were committed to engaging parents as decision-makers in the planning and implementation of work at the centre. They knew that working in this way was not about compensating for disadvantage. Instead it was about acknowledging the impact of poverty on the lives of local children and their families, and encouraging families to take an equal and active role in developing responsive services.

The principles that underpin the work at Pen Green are the principles of community education. Community education should:

- be concerned with the individuals' capacity to be self directing;
- help individuals to gain more control over their lives;
- be about raising self-esteem;
- promote learning as a lifelong experience;
- be about equal opportunities;
- be about pushing boundaries;

- be about constructive discontent – not having to put up with things the way they are;
- encourage people to feel they have the power to change things; and
- be about self-fulfilment (adapted from Whalley, 1994).

A one-stop shop

Chris Athey (1990) describes the conceptual gulf that exists when groups of people who lack shared experience begin to work together. The newly appointed staff at Pen Green adopted an 'open door' approach which helped to bridge the gap between these local parents and the new service. Parents were invited into the centre before the concrete was even dry. They shared the experience of transforming a derelict comprehensive school, which many of them had attended, into a stimulating and secure environment for very young children and their families. They shared the responsibility for establishing priorities, allocating space and developing the work.

Over the next 14 years the centre developed the following strands of activity:

Early years education.
Extended hours, extended year provision to support families.
Inclusive, flexible, education with care for children in need and children with special educational needs.
Adult community education and family support services.
Voluntary work and community regeneration.
Training and support for early years practitioners.
Research and development.

The centre became a 'one-stop shop' for families with young children in the local community (Audit Commission, 1994). What we at the centre provided for children and families was as follows:

- a high-quality developmentally appropriate early childhood education with care provision for young children;
- a place where children could meet, learn and grow, where staff worked hard to meet children's affective and cognitive needs, where there was appropriate provision for children in need;
- an inclusive service for children with special educational needs;
- a seamless provision for parents with accessible adult education, health and social welfare services all on one site; the centre became

a focus for lifelong learning in the community; and
- a centre where parents were engaged in an equal, active and responsible partnership, and shared their concerns about their children's development.

The changing political agenda

By 1997 the need to involve parents actively in their children's education was high on the political agenda of the newly elected Labour government. Two of the main reasons for this were that the role of parents as their children's first and most consistent educators was by now firmly established (Barber, 1996, p. 244). The link between parents' own experiences of the education system, their attitudes and expectations and their children's achievement was also acknowledged as a factor of even greater significance than school improvement (OECD, 1997).

In 1997 the government made recommendations that there should be a fully integrated approach to early years education and care across the public, private and voluntary sector. Supporting parents and training parents were identified as major tasks for early childhood educators in all settings (DfEE, 1996; DfEE, 1997).

Early excellence centres

In December 1997 the government launched its Centres of Excellence programmes (DfEE, 1997) offering financial support and defining standards for those individual centres or networks where flexible, high-quality early years education and care were offered alongside education and training for parents. This government initiative acted as a catalyst, inspiring many local authorities to bid for funding to improve existing services or to initiate projects.

Pen Green was one of the first centres designated by the government as a Centre of Excellence. The additional financial support the centre received meant that we could increase our educational services to both children and their parents with new after-school programmes for school-aged children and for family education. The government acknowledged the work of the centre in providing local and national training: 'The centre is . . . a focal point for training early years educators in the public, private and voluntary sectors and is playing a major role in the dissemination of good practice in early years provision' (DfEE, 1998, p. 19). Under the Early Excellence Programme Pen Green was allocated funding for a new Family Education annex which provided badly needed accommodation and space in which to set up our research and development work.

Education action zones

Another government initiative that had an immediate impact on the Pen Green Centre and on Corby was the establishment of Education Action Zones. Early Action Zones (EAZs) were set up to galvanize local schools and improve educational achievement. Most EAZs focused on work in the secondary phase but some had an early years component. All EAZs had a primary task the raising of parental expectations. Data generated from the schools in Corby in 1997 identified the area as one in which children were significantly under-achieving. Corby had three schools in special measures and in 1999 was declared an Education Action Zone.

Statistics showed that there were very few adults in Corby who had undertaken further or higher education and this was confirmed by interviews that we had completed with parents using the centre. Eighteen out of the 22 parents who completed our interview schedules had left school at, or before, age 16. The majority of the parents who responded felt that 'school had not brought out the best in them'. Perhaps because so few parents in Corby have continued their education post 16, and because most parents experienced education as a disempowering force in their own lives, a culture of low expectations had developed.

Corby Sure Start

In 1999 the government introduced another major initiative, the national Sure Start Programme (DfEE, 1999a). This programme was designed to offer comprehensive support to families with children under 4 years in disadvantaged neighbourhoods. A Sure Start Unit accountable to both the Minister for Health and the Minister for Education was set up. Identified communities were invited to prepare proposals for innovative multidisciplinary work. The programme had a strong community development strand and there was an expectation that local people would be involved in developing local bids.

Pen Green became the lead partner for Corby Sure Start and worked in collaboration with all the other statutory and voluntary agencies concerned with family support. A particular feature of the Corby Sure Start programme was that large numbers of parents were involved in conceptualizing the local targets and programmes of work. Parents who had been involved in Pen Green for several years became powerful advocates for other parents living in the extended catchment area that was the 'Sure Start Community'. A parent-led needs assessment was immediately set up to assess the effectiveness of local services for the 103 new families whose children were born in the previous year. Parents were recruited, paid and trained in interview techniques. They constructed an interview schedule collaboratively with staff and then went out and conducted informal interviews (Pen Green Research Report, 2000). This provided rich data for the new Sure Start programme, data which were analysed and then shared with local agencies. Parents presented the data at local seminars and conferences and professionals were able to use very creatively the constructive feedback they were given. Within a few months professionals were already beginning to make services more accessible and responsive to families.

A learning community

By the late 1990s what we had created at Pen Green was an environment in which:

- children, parents and staff were encouraged to be good decision-makers, able to question, challenge and make choices;
- there were opportunities for staff to become highly trained reflective practitioners, with good levels of support and supervision, in an environment where they could build satisfactory relationships and feel valued personally and professionally;
- staff consulted with and felt accountable to all the stakeholders – children, parents, staff, the local community, the LEA and local authority; and
- parents had become advocates for their children and were beginning to share their understanding of their children's learning at home with nursery staff.

Over 17 years we had been able to develop a comprehensive parent partnership programme. More than 6,000 local parents had been involved (Whalley, 1997) and staff had established a model of co-operative working that respected both the learning and support needs of parents, and the children's right to high-quality early years education with care.

Our work with parents was underpinned by the belief that all parents had a critical role to play as their child's primary educators. We were aware that young children achieve more and are happier when early years educators work together with parents and share views on how to support and extend children's learning (Athey, 1990; Meade, 1995). The belief that parents' involvement should be a key feature of any high-quality early years provision has been well supported in government reports from the Plowden Report in 1967 to *Excellence in Schools* in 1997 (DfEE, 1997).

The concept of a 'triangle of care' was developed in the Start Right report (Ball, 1994) which described a new kind of partnership between parents and professionals. Through this equal and active partnership a secure, warm and stimulating environment could be created for children. Parents, for the first time, were described as having their own 'proper competences' and parents' deep commitment to their children's learning was finally acknowledged.

The Start Right report made it clear that the key issue for early childhood educators in education and care settings was to develop a strong relationship with parents as the child's first and enduring educators. The role of early childhood settings was to support parents through:

- exemplifying good practice;
- providing information about current research;
- offering appropriate parent education and professional support; and
- helping parents to develop and sustain their sense of self-esteem and self-efficacy.

Research showed that a large number of parents wanted to be involved in their children's early school experiences (Smith, 1990). The involvement of parents in the Froebel Early Education Project (1973–78) provided evidence of deep commitment on the part of parents who were consulted on professional concerns rather than 'peripheral issues' (Athey, 1990, p. 206).

Research also indicated that children made significant gains when their parents were involved in early childhood programmes (Lazar, 1983). However, researchers were still unclear about just 'how' parental involvement actually benefits children in nursery settings (Meade, 1995).

Setting up a research base in an early excellence centre

Building on our long tradition of parental involvement we decided in 1996 to establish a research base at Pen Green in partnership with parents, early years practitioners and researchers in high education. We realized we had underestimated the enthusiasm which parents demonstrated for a deeper and more extended dialogue about their children's learning. We began to see that teaching and learning and curriculum issues, which had previously been the fairly uncontested domain of professional staff, needed to be opened up for a wider discussion with parents in the early years community.

What we needed was a rich and relevant dialogue between parents and nursery staff which could be sustained over time, a dialogue which focused on the children's learning and achievements and our own pedagogic practice.

2

Developing Evidence-Based Practice

Margy Whalley

> I would like to see the research world opening its doors much more fully to practice and practitioners, embracing the messy chaotic world of the young child and trying to work with it in order to understand it more fully.
>
> (Pascal, 1996, p. 5)

As a committed group of reflective practitioners concerned with both institutional development and professional development, staff at Pen Green had naturally developed a commitment to the research process. Because the service we were offering was innovatory, there was a great deal of interest in the centre both from social scientists and educationalists in universities and research institutions in the UK and overseas. Staff, parents and children grew accustomed to being the object of other people's research programmes. These research exercises helped us to become better informed practitioners. At Pen Green the staff, like early childhood educators in Reggio Emilia and in Sweden (Edwards, Gandini and Forman, 1998), are convinced that 'pedagogic practice demands continuous adaptation and reflection if it is to evolve' (Dahlberg, at 1998 seminar). Although these research exercises helped us to become better informed practitioners, being the objects of research rather than participants in it proved to be problematic at times.

Our early years curriculum has evolved dynamically over the years and is very much concerned with the 'researching child' capable of performing 'heroic feats' (Dahlberg, 1998). We worked hard to encourage the children to become effective decision-makers, able to reflect deeply on their own experiences. We also encouraged staff to become more reflective practitioners. Increasingly, because of their involvement with higher education and further education studies and our centre-based in-service training programme, staff took on small-scale action research projects addressing their own questions and con-

11

cerns. These in the main were concerned with children's development and parental involvement (Arnold, 1990, 1999; Malcolm, 1993). Staff learnt a great deal from these small-scale research projects about children's well-being, their learning strategies and the importance of observation. They also developed a deeper understanding of the kinds of intervention that women valued as parents and why fathers found it harder to get involved. The fact that all staff consistently received high levels of support and supervision made it possible for them to receive critical input, from parents and colleagues and visitors, and to be positively self-critical without feeling overwhelmed by guilt when things were not going well.

At this stage the decision was made that we should formalize our research partnerships with our critical friends from higher education institutions and with the children and their parents (Hargreaves, 1996). We decided to start taking ourselves more seriously as practitioner researchers. In 1995/96 we established a small-scale, research development and training base with two key research posts. Funding, in the first instance, came from income generated by training and development work and, subsequently, from a research grant.

Our aims in this new research were to:

- develop an effective dialogue with parents about their children's learning at home and at nursery;
- develop a style of working with parents, that empowers rather than de-skills;
- develop a greater understanding of how parents were encouraging their children to learn at home;
- compare and contrast the styles that nursery staff and parents adopt when engaging children in learning experiences; and
- produce materials to assist parents to get actively involved in recording and understanding their children's development.

Partners not victims

Building on our own previous experience we felt it was important that the research was not about doing things to people. We wanted to adopt a research methodology where the forms of investigation were enabling and participative. Young families and early years practitioners are both marginalized groups, often living on low incomes. A large number of the families using Pen Green have no choice but to depend on welfare benefit and welfare services. Bob Holman (1987) makes the point that research is largely about, on or for the poor and is rarely designed or written by, or with, the poor. One of the central concerns of our research was that it would help families living in poverty. Throughout the life of the project we were concerned with involving parents as equal and active partners in the research process. We adopted a timescale and methodology which was acceptable to them. In this way, our research project fits the category that Holman (1987) defines as 'research from the underside'.

We also made it clear to parents that this research was not undertaken with the view that the parenting they were demonstrating was of a 'deficit model'. Our experience was that the parents using the nursery at Pen Green had a passionate commitment to their children. Their deep insight into their own children's development had often provided nursery staff with essential information. In this way parents had helped us to develop a more effective pedagogical approach, and a more relevant and responsive curriculum.

Our shared code of ethics was as follows. Research at Pen Green should always:

* be positive for all the participants;
* provide data that are open to, accountable to and interpreted by all the participants;
* focus on questions that the participants themselves (parents and children and staff) are asking;
* be based on a relationship of trust where people's answers are believed; and
* produce results which are about improving practice at home and at nursery, or at least sustaining it.

First attempts at involving parents, 1995

Our initial dialogue with parents about their involvement in their children's learning was fairly unfocused. During this period nursery parents were encouraged to keep records of their children's play and development at home, using diaries and video cameras. Small numbers of parents got involved. Often parents found it difficult to decide what was noteworthy. Whilst a few parents made insightful observations of their children playing at home which were very useful for nursery staff, other parents simply recorded amusing incidents or family events such as birthday parties. Parents behaved like nursery staff when they first used the camcorder and tended to go for quantity rather than quality. That summer we had more than 30 hours of video tape to watch and analyse. Parents were also hungry for feedback. Although these vignettes of family life helped parents to maintain a creative dialogue with nursery staff and gave us useful information about the children's rich social lives, they did not help us to consistently support and extend the children's learning in the nursery.

Having a second 'shot', 1996: parents and early childhood educators engaging children in learning

With new funding from the Teacher Training Agency (Whalley and Arnold, 1997a), we spent five months looking closely at the different ways that nursery staff and parents engaged with the children in the nursery. Initially we worked with a group of ten families who had already shown an interest in their children's development through discussions with the nursery staff. The families involved were all going to be using the nursery during the summer holidays and throughout the following academic year, and were all able to commit time to the project. They included employed and unemployed parents, single parents, reconstituted families where one parent was a step-parent, married and unmarried couples. Eight of the families were white European. Two parents were from minority ethnic groups.

At the first informal meeting between parents, nursery staff and research staff the parents were asked if they were willing to be videotaped settling their children into nursery and playing alongside their children at the beginning of the day. The parents were also asked if they would keep a diary (or make an audiotape) about how their children played at home. We discussed with them their willingness to either let staff video them at home or help them set up the video so that they could film themselves interacting with their child. It was important that all the parents made their own decisions about the nature and level of their involvement.

Developing a shared language

> Teachers of young children could make a revolutionary move forward in developing a pedagogy of the early years if they recorded how they conceptualised and shared their professional concepts with parents.
>
> (Athey, 1990, p. 206)

It seemed to us that if parents were to be able to enter into a dialogue about their children's learning, then nursery staff and parents needed to have a' shared conceptual framework. We felt it was essential to spend time developing this framework for thinking with parents, not because there is only one way to think about learning and teaching but because it is critically important to develop a shared language with parents (Drummond, 1989; Dahlberg, Moss and Pence, 1999). Using a shared language we could discuss the ways in which children learn and how adults can effectively intervene to support and extend children's learning. When adults intervene they adopt a particular pedagogical approach and this approach is underpinned by a particular philosophy. At Pen Green our philosophy is that early childhood educators are interactionists (Bruce, 1997, p. 10). They base their interventions on careful observations of the children, they spend time watching children and work alongside the child to support and extend their learning, they teach skills when appropriate, they reflect deeply and make links between child development theory and their own practice.

When we observe the children in the nursery at Pen Green we also do so from within a conceptual framework. We set up training sessions to help parents find a focus for their observations of their children at home, sharing with them our understanding of the work of Susan Isaacs at the Malting House (Isaacs, 1936), whose open-ended observations and celebration of children's cognitive competence had made a real impact on our staff group. In Chapter 8, this approach is described in more detail.

Deep-level learning

In one of the training sessions we explained to the parents how we used the Leuven Involvement Scale in our observations of children in the nursery (Laevers, 1994). We shared our understanding of this scale, which is not designed to make judgements about children's performance, but rather as a tool to assess whether the provision that adults are offering to the child is sufficiently stimulating to support and extend their learning: 'the child's closely focused attention usually suggests that a good match has been made between an adult's stimulus and some particular or general concern in the child' (Athey, 1990, p. 63). When a child is 'deeply involved' he or she scores 4–5 on the scale. The provision is appropriate and the pedagogical approach is supportive. When the child is scoring at a low level then there is something wrong with the provision, the adult may be intervening inappropriately or the child's well-being may be low.

Parents found these sessions fascinating and quickly picked up the idea that if their children were deeply involved then it would be appropriate to record what they were doing using the camcorder or their diaries. Chris Athey comments on how the parents in the Froebel Early Education Project responded in a similar vein: 'Nothing gets under a parents' skin more quickly and more permanently than the illumination of his or her own child's behaviour. The effect of participation can be profound' (Athey, 1990, p. 66).

Adult engagement styles

The parents became equally absorbed in a subsequent training session on adult engagement styles (Pascal and Bertram, 1997). The Adult Engagement Style is a methodology designed to assess the adults' ability to engage children effectively in a learning situation. It is described in detail in the work of Pascal and Bertram, who direct the National Effective Early Learning Project. Staff at Pen Green, who had been involved in the Effective Early Learning project since 1993, were accustomed to recording the way that adults in a nursery interacted with children in terms of the degree to which they stimulated the children and the sensitivity with which they engaged them. We wanted parents to have the same kind of information and understanding as staff about these *pedagogical* approaches.

In Chapter 4 Cath Arnold describes in much more detail the training sessions that we set up and makes suggestions as to how these concepts could be shared in other settings.

What we all learnt: levels of commitment vary

Parents were given a lot of time and space to express their anxieties about the research project in general, and the training programme in particular. All ten parents got involved on their own terms. Some could only commit to a few fairly evenly spaced meetings in the evening. Others were keen to keep diaries, make video recordings and work with staff on a daily basis. Our job was to use the time the parents were willing to spend with us to good effect.

We learnt not to make simplistic judgements about parents' commitment to the project on the basis of how often they showed up or the material that they brought with them. All the parents were deeply concerned about their children. We soon realized that we had to plan meetings very carefully around work shifts. Running meetings in the evenings with a creche so that parents had no anxieties about childcare, and providing a meal to ensure energy and conviviality often worked best.

For one or two of the parents this was the first time that they had become deeply involved in work at the centre. For example, Sardi, Zaki's mother, had spent enormous amounts of time with her son in

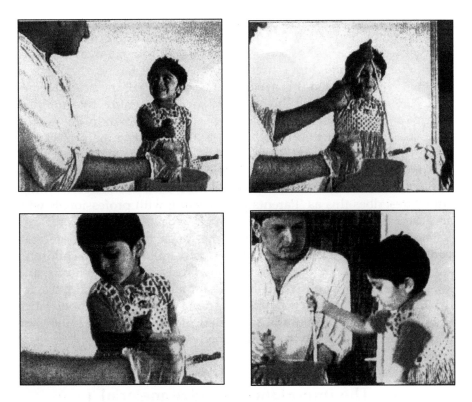

Figure 2.1 Zaki filmed at home

the nursery and had become a regular parent/helper (she subsequently went on to train as a paid crèche worker). Abid, Zaki's father, was unable to spend much time in the nursery because of his work commitments. Abid had a deep interest in his son's learning and joined a group of fathers attending an evening course on early literacy issues. During the research project, Abid became very involved in attending evening meetings, sharing his views and using the camcorder at home. Some of the richest video clips that parents brought us were of Zaki and his father chatting in Urdu and English and mixing up paste to decorate their kitchen (Figure 2.1). Abid clearly understands the importance of Zaki's 'rotation' schema and is feeding his interest in stirring things with appropriate curriculum content (Athey, 1990, p. 203).

Abid encourages Zaki, who is 3½ years old, to rotate the screwdriver and attempt to repair a door hinge; he encourages Zaki to mix the paste (Zaki refers to this as making the dinner) and allows him to deconstruct and then repair a trolley by unscrewing and then screwing back on all of its eight wheels. Each of the beautifully video-filmed learning sequences made by Sardi show Zaki on his own or, more often, deeply engaged in activities with Abid his father.

When we completed this project nine out of ten of the original families had sustained their involvement over the entire five months. Despite the fact that three marriages had broken down in this period only one couple felt that they had to withdraw from the project as a result of this marital conflict.

Working in this way parents developed strong relationships with nursery staff and gained new insights into their children's learning. Athey describes this as 'Parents participating with professionals with an articulated pedagogy' (Athey, 1990, p. 50).

The nursery curriculum also became much richer and more relevant because it increasingly acknowledged and built on the children's learning at home. Although we had previously made home visits, and knew a great deal about the children's social and emotional lives, for the first time the focus was on cognition. We began to know much more about what excited and interested the children and could then plan to support and extend their interests in the nursery to great effect.

The importance of video material

Videos of the children

Evening meetings were always well attended by parents, particularly when video clips of their own children were to be viewed and discussed. In Chapter 7 we look closely at the way in which parents developed insights into their children's learning and shared their understandings with staff through attending study groups and making and watching tapes.

Videos of the adults engaging with the children

Parents and nursery staff wanted clear boundaries set with regard to watching videos which had been made of adults interacting with children in the nursery and in home settings. Parents were clearly anxious that staff might watch the videos and make judgements or formulate opinions about the parents' interventions without having heard the parents' perspective. Nursery staff had the same kind of anxieties. They were very happy to agree that the analysis of the video should be a shared activity. However, once again we had completely underestimated how much video footage the project would generate. During this period we made 24 hours' footage and this included for the first time home video material.

The quality of these tapes was very high and they made rich and rewarding viewing. The children were almost always learning at a deep level. Parents seemed to have put to good use their training sessions on the Leuven Involvement Scale and made well-informed decisions about what was worth videoing. Subsequently, they made informed decisions about what kind of provision to make for their children in the home.

Since we were committed to offering training to all parents who expressed an interest in getting more involved in their children's learning we decided that it would be useful to produce a CD-ROM as a training tool. By carefully selecting video clips from home and nursery and matching them with a simple text it was possible for us to communicate and share complex and dynamic ideas with parents (Whalley and Whalley, 1996). The CD-ROM demonstrated both the complexity and the intimacy of the relationships between parents, nursery staff and children and the rich dialogue that had been established in a fairly short time between all the partners in this project. It is used in-house regularly by parents, particularly fathers, nursery staff and visitors.

One riveting sequence on the CD-ROM was made by staff who were allowed to film Sean, aged 3, and his father, John, at home. John first allowed staff to film, and then taught himself how to set up the camcorder. He made some gripping home movies of Sean learning to subdivide space by cutting up bread with a fairly sharp knife. Through John's tapes we began to appreciate the extent to which parents were taking on their role as parent-educators. This helped us to put into perspective the relatively small contribution that we make to any child's life as early childhood educators.

When Sean was not in the nursery he was still learning all the time; his father took him on long walks each day with his dog. John carried Sean in a pannier and went on cycle rides to visit derelict manor houses, and to tea dances with the old folks at the home. He took Sean on trade union marches and down to the park as part of his daily routine. Challenged by other project parents as to how safe it really was to take his son to the park which was full of 'winos', dog faeces and refuse, John responded that his son knew all the 'winos' by name and that he was bringing him up to be a socialist soldier.

Mainstreaming the work: extending the programme to the whole nursery, 1997–2000

We had learnt a great deal and all the nursery staff were deeply committed to sustaining a dialogue with parents. We knew that it would be important to develop an approach that could become part of everyday nursery practice. Working with the parents we negotiated the aims of the project.

Our aims for the children were to:

- value each child's individuality, enhance each child's self-esteem and to identify the cognitive concerns of all the children in the nursery;
- generate stimulating curriculum content particularly in areas that are sometimes neglected in the the early years, for example, mathematics and science; and
- extend the impact of the research and development work to younger siblings in the home.

For the parents our aims were to:

- encourage parents to observe and understand how and what their children are learning at home;
- acknowledge the skills and competencies of parents and build on these to enhance our own pedagogical strategies;
- encourage parents to feel equal and active in their involvement, and to develop an information exchange as a two-way process; and
- provide accessible and relevant routes into involvement so that *all* families using the nursery feel informed about their children's development – for example, fathers as well as mothers, isolated vulnerable parents, and parents who are traditionally 'hard to reach'.

For the nursery staff and other early childhood educators our aims were to:

- make it possible for all the nursery staff to become 'practitioner researchers' able to debate issues amongst themselves, to articulate their understanding of theory and practice, and to develop a genuine dialogue with parents; and
- share the parents and nursery staff's knowledge and experience with as wide an audience as possible.

The children's perspective

The philosophy of our nursery has always been that the curriculum should encourage children to have high self-esteem and a strong sense of self-efficacy. Since 'children's expectations may be more influential in their learning than their ability' (Smiley and Dweck, 1994). Like Rutter (1997) we believe resilience should be seen as an outcome of education.

Children can become very effective decision-makers. They need to be able to plan and translate their plans into actions (Laevers, 1995). They also need to hypothesize and experiment. If we are to help them develop this sense of mastery then it is critically important that we take children's central cognitive concerns as a starting point for our nursery curriculum (Sylva, 1994). Children's thinking is characterized by their ability to, 'conceptualise and consolidate' (Handy, quoted in Scott, 1997, p. 4).

Parents and nursery staff, who are important adults in young children's lives, need to be centrally concerned with the provision of a rich and challenging curriculum. 'The development of co-ordinating complexities of thinking must be cultivated and fleshed out from birth in the home and in the school' (Athey, 1990, p. 206).

Nursery staff worked hard to match their observations of the children with those of the parents. Each member of staff took responsibility for reading and reviewing the diary entries that parents brought in from home and the video vignettes that some parents offered us. All nursery staff met together each week and matched the parents' observations with those made in the nursery by the staff team. With both sets of information curriculum planning in the nursery became much more focused and we were able to respond quickly to individual children. Staff developed the workshop environments within the nursery so that children could 'service themselves' and access almost all the materials independently.

Autonomy

Nursery staff were convinced that developing a sense of autonomy was important for children. We worked closely with the parents and the children to develop a shared understanding of autonomy:

- an action that has been freely chosen;
- where the child willingly self-regulates;
- for which the child accepts full responsibility;
- which is based on personal conviction, and is not simply about obedience (Burk-Rogers, 1998).

The Pen Green nursery team and the parents became 'autonomy supporting educators'. We shared the belief that offering children choices was critically important and that the choices 'should be geared to the children's level of involvement' (Burk-Rogers, 1998, p. 77). We knew different members of the nursery staff encouraged children to be autonomous in different ways and to different degrees (Bertram, 1995). We also knew that there were big differences between rules, boundaries and the level of choice offered to children at home and at nursery (Nucci and Smetana, 1996). Staff set up groups to establish parents' views on autonomy and to find ways to encourage children to make decisions and choices in nursery. These focused discussions provided rich material for debate in staff meetings.

Boys being boys

Over a number of years nursery staff had noticed that from January to March, a small group of 4-year-old boys would emerge who appeared to be less engaged and tended to behave problematically. This was often the case even when the boys concerned had previously shown consistently high levels of involvement. Each year staff tried different strategies to engage these boys but without much success, and their behaviour had been interpreted by nursery staff as some kind of 'rite of transition' – a need to be assertive before entry into primary school.

In January 1998, at the end of the first year of the 'mainstreamed' project, for the first time, staff noticed that this pattern of behaviour did not occur. The group of 4-year-old boys due to move on to primary school in September remained deeply involved. We speculated that this was because we were matching their cognitive needs with a much richer curriculum content heavily weighted, probably for the first time, towards mathematics and science.

Becoming scientists and mathematicians

Over the five years of the project the children's hypothesizing became increasingly complex. We became aware that as early years educators we needed further in-service training in the areas of mathematics and science; relatively few of us had qualifications, extensive experience or confidence in these curriculum areas. As our understanding of children's home concerns and nursery concerns has developed we have continued to make greater provision for science and mathematics in the nursery. We set up in-service training days in 1998 which focused on these aspects of the curriculum so that staff felt better able to respond to children's fascination with levers, pulleys, gravity, rotation, spheres and trajectories. In Chapter 8 we see the impact this had on girls as well as boys.

Pen Green discovery area

By 1999 nursery staff were working with architects, designers, manufacturers and educational consultants to develop a new science discovery area. This was funded in part by the DfEE and through our own fund-raising efforts. Our decision-making process was heavily informed by watching the nursery children in a number of different settings. Initially we took them, with their parents, to the Science Museum in London where they investigated water channels, wheat chutes and used conveyor belts. Subsequently, we gave the children opportunities to experiment with a range of equipment in schools and parks. For example, we took a small group of children to Chatsworth Park to experiment with a range of outdoor play equipment. Our children found the Archimedes Screw too hard to turn and staff discovered that the flow of water from the local stream fed insufficient water into the system for it to present any challenge to children. Time was well spent in reconnaissance.

Perhaps the most important part of this planning stage was time spent in discussion with each other as a nursery team. We knew from our extensive observations of children in nursery that what was needed was a stimulating and challenging environment, where, through effective interactions with staff and their peers, children's thinking and hypothesizing could be supported and extended. Initially, we focused on concepts that the children were already exploring in the nursery and identified aspects of the new provision that might enhance their learning. We wanted the children to feel that they were in control of the new equipment and that they could make independent decisions about how it was used. 'Returning to the bedrock education principles, children need to actively learn, physically through movement. If they can't make equipment work by themselves, they become frustrated and the curriculum becomes one of "can't do". Self motivation is damaged. Autonomy turns to dependency on adults for help' (Bruce, 1999).

The physical environment was designed in such a way that through sound, light, texture and colour, children's aesthetic, kinesthetic and emotional needs were satisfied (Ceppi and Zini, 1998). In this way we celebrated our pedagogy and our understanding of children's learning styles through the architecture (Figure 2.2). This discovery area offered children a much enhanced provision including a very deep and large sandpit with a conveyor belt, horizontal and vertical pul-

Figure 2.2 Discovery area

leys with visible workings. It also contained a complex system of water chutes that could be dammed and flooded, where the water flow could be directed by the children. With additional support from the DfEE we invested in closed-circuit television (CCTV) cameras so that we could record the use of this equipment, study the way that this new provision supported and extended children's learning and consolidate and reflect on our pedagogical approaches (Pen Green/DfEE, 1999).

Supporting siblings

In 1996 and 1997 the project parents noted that the insights they had gained from child development theory and sharing ideas with other parents, and their own nursery children's learning, had a direct impact on younger siblings in the family. This impact on siblings was a strong feature of the Froebel Early Education Project (Athey, 1990, p. 56). As a staff group, we knew that 'rich experiences really do produce rich brains' (Nash, 1997, p. 37; Blakemore, 1998) which is why it seemed critical to us that we should be making direct links with children from birth to 3-years-old as well as with nursery-aged children: 'the early months, never mind the early years of a child's life are critical to their life chances' (Barber, 1996, p. 244).

In 1998, by popular demand, two baby and toddler study groups were set up which were co-led by parents and staff who had been involved in the nursery parents' study groups. Both groups were called 'Growing Together' groups and were always full. Unlike the nursery parent study groups parents attended the Growing Together groups *with* their babies and toddlers. These parents were offered the same training sessions in child development concepts as the nursery parents, and an additional training session on using the video camera.

Within each session parents were encouraged to observe and support their children's learning. The provision included treasure baskets (Goldschmied, 1991) and heuristic play materials as well as water, sand and playdough.

Parents became increasingly confident in using the video to record important learning moments at home and brought these video vignettes to the session. Within the sessions staff videoed interesting learning sequences and printed them out through the computer so that parents could take them home to show to partners or grandparents (see Figure 2.3).

Figure 2.3 Lucy's learning sequence

The parents' perspective

Parents using the nursery had demonstrated a deep commitment to supporting and nurturing their children in the pilot project. They had shown us that it was possible for parents who had everything stacked against them in terms of socio-economic status, lack of educational achievement and low levels of family support to become very effective advocates for their children. Since 'Parents' expectations are the most powerful predictor of children's later school success' (Bredekamp and Shepherd, 1989, p. 22) we knew that it would be important to sustain and extend the programme.

Different parents: different approaches

Since parents are all very different we were aware that we needed to offer parents a range of 'ways in' to the project. Some parents had time during the day and valued the opportunities we offered to share problems and anxieties with other parents in study groups that ran for a year or more. In these groups they would discuss their children's cognitive concerns and share problems and perceptions regarding their child's social and emotional needs. Parents' diary entries, nursery observations and video vignettes of the children in nursery were used to inform these sessions. Sometimes parents would bring in the video tapes they had made at home. By 1999 33 per cent of parents had borrowed the video camera and brought in vignettes of their children playing and learning at home, and nursery staff had made ten videotapes and sent them out to parents, when parents or partners could not come into the nursery.

Other parents attended a monthly evening meeting. We tried to make each of these evening sessions a self-contained discussion group. During the day parents were asked to fill in a reply slip to say whether they would be attending that night or not. If we knew they were coming, then video vignettes of their children were made in the nursery. These short video clips formed the basis for sharing information in the evening session about their child's learning needs.

In Chapter 3 Colette Tait describes the many strategies we developed to encourage parents to take part. Nursery staff made no assumptions about commitment on the basis of attendance at meetings. We observed parents who after only attending one training session managed to maintain high levels of involvement, keeping home diaries and sharing this information with nursery staff and video filming at home even when they could not physically attend meetings at the nursery on a regular basis. The issue of attrition was critically important to us and we wanted to encourage parents to sustain their involvement over time. However, we knew that pressures of parenting, tiredness, anxiety, work commitments, practical difficulties like access and babysitting would often create difficulties for parents.

Involving fathers

Getting in touch with fathers was sometimes a problem. We have always had a policy of regular home visiting before the child starts nursery, and then three times a year as a general rule. However, many of the nursery children were living in reconstituted families and in several cases fathers had no contact with their biological children. In other cases, when parents had separated acrimoniously, fathers were not informed about what was happening in their children's lives at nursery. Often staff did not have fathers' addresses, and all contact was through the child's mother. Additionally, even where mothers and fathers were living together, some mothers told us that they censored information coming from the nursery because they thought it would not be important, or appropriate, for the child's father to be involved. We clearly could not afford to be gender neutral in developing this project.

Involving fathers or male carers is, however, a complex issue. Staff at Pen Green have had some degree of success in engaging fathers in practical ways in the past (Whalley, 1998). Encouraging fathers to sustain their involvement over time has been more problematic (Chandler, 1997). In Chapter 5 we consider in more detail the new ways in which staff have worked to consistently engage fathers.

Direct work with parents who are isolated, vulnerable or distrustful of 'the system'

We were aware in the early stages of the pilot project that there were some women attending sessions who had an overwhelming need to talk about themselves and what was going on in their lives even when the group had as its focus children's learning and development. Since there are many groups at the centre which offer support to isolated, depressed and vulnerable families, these parents sometimes simply 'dropped out' of the research project and joined a therapeutic or support group where the focus was, more appropriately, on their adult needs (Whalley, 1997b). There was also a small number of mothers who did not appear to benefit from the experience of meeting and sharing with others information about their children's development. These women although initially enthusiastic tended to withdraw after two or three sessions. Most of these women had been excluded from school and had left school before the age of 16.

We sensed that it might be particularly important to engage both these groups of women since they often had older children who were struggling and failing in the primary or secondary phase. However if these parents were to accept any form of intervention (Oakley *et al.*, 1995) then it had to be offered on an individual basis. Some of these women were experiencing extremes of poverty or social isolation because of drug usage, or because there were professional concerns about child protection issues. Others were suffering from depression, perhaps as a result of emotional or sexual abuse in childhood. Janet Shaw (1991) describes in detail the effectiveness of individual work with such parents and the importance of sustained home visiting.

Shaw's work makes it clear that it is possible, and indeed essential, to encourage parents in these circumstances to become involved in their children's learning. In Chapter 8 Cath Arnold describes at some length interventions that worked with women who were fairly distrustful of the 'system'.

The impact on parents

All the parents involved in this project were asked to fill in a questionnaire which was concerned with the impact of the project on their relationship with their child. *Most* parents reported significant changes in the way that they responded to their child. *All* the parents commented on their increased understanding of the learning potential there was in everyday experiences. *Most* reported that being involved in the project had changed the way that they selected books, toys and Christmas and birthday presents for their children.

The following account is an extract from one parents' feedback on the impact of the project.

Louise C:

At home Philip is very demanding – I have to be no more than a few inches away from him most of the time, and when I do get to be in a different room from him, he checks on me every few minutes. Since taking part in the research project, I try to find things that interest him, so that when I'm washing up or making the beds or just cooking dinner, he has things to do that hold his interest long enough for me to do what I've got to do.

Since the project started, I've learnt to be a bit more tolerant about the mess they make (most of the time). They have learnt that there are places where they can paint and draw (in the dining room), and that as long as they keep to the few rules that I try to make them keep, I allow them a bit more leeway, i.e. I won't tidy up the table if they are halfway through colouring or drawing a picture, I'll leave it until they get home from school.

When Allan and I were trying to work out what they would get for Christmas, we did try to link with what Philip did in nursery – we bought him a fishing game (which he plays with most days), playdough, lots of cutters. He also got a small parcel with stickers, sellotape, glue, scissors and paper shapes. Allan wasn't sure about these, but they were a big hit. We also bought things they had particularly asked for, but these haven't been played with as much. It has also made me realize that toys are not always the most obvious things for him to play with. Philip will often empty the drawer with all the plastic dishes, and play with them for a long time. One of the 'toys' he likes best, is the egg timer he wanted me to buy. He has had a lot of fun with that and it is never far away from his favourite toys.

Having the videos has helped to keep family and friends up to date. His Grandma feels she misses such a lot since he started full-time nursery, it's nice to show her videos of what he's doing.

For me, it is good to know that Philip is no better or worse behaved than many other children. It is nice to know that other people have the same problems, and to know that your child is developing normally. I hope that he will continue with these friendships he has already made.

It has made me think about the things I do with the boys – I would never have thought to take Philip to the Science Museum, but he had a great time, and took in more than I would have expected him to. Keeping his diary has helped to show me how he has developed and grown and changed – although it is only by going back and reading it that I can see it.

It just seems a shame that there will not be a similar project at school – it would be interesting to see how he develops, but I can appreciate that there are too many children and not enough teachers to tailor a child's education.

For me it has been good to know that other parents get cross, upset and annoyed at their children and all that any parent can do is love their child always – unconditionally.

A catalyst for training and adult learning

Many parents who have been involved in the research and development project have also gone on to undertake accredited training in childcare and other subjects. Some have gone on to become childcare workers. Having attended a research study group for one to two years, a number of project parents have gone on to undertake a City and Guilds crèche worker course at Pen Green Centre, or to qualify through the National Vocational Qualification (NVQ) route (Pen Green Centre is an assessment centre for the delivery of NVQs in Education and Childcare).

For example, there were ten parents in the Tuesday afternoon study group; of these, the following seven parents have gone on to undertake training or to run childcare services in a voluntary or paid capacity:

Rosanna – works as a volunteer co-leading a weekly baby massage group and has undertaken paid work as a research worker for the Sure Start project and is now running groups for the Sure Start Project.

Dave – works voluntarily in the Pen Green Nursery and has embarked on his NVQ level III in Childcare. He also works full time at night.

Lesley – has completed NVQ level III in Childcare and is now employed 15 hours a week in Pen Green Nursery, working with children with special needs. Lesley also has paid work in the local primary school.

Carole – has gained an A Grade in English A-level, has undertaken four weeks' supply work in nursery and now has paid work in a local primary school.

Louise – works as a childcare worker at a local sports centre, having previously undertaken home study in Childcare. She is a paid co-leader of one of the Growing Together study groups and is currently completing her NVQ level III at Pen Green.

Eloise – works as a volunteer co-leading a weekly parent and toddler play session and has paid work as a member of the kitchen staff.

Tracey – has undertaken and passed A-level English and works part time outside the centre.

The nursery staff perspective

Mainstreaming the work in the nursery

Our key concern as the research project developed was to see whether what we had achieved could be sustained and consolidated within Pen Green's early childhood setting. For example, by 1998 we had 84 per cent of nursery families involved in the programme. Not only were these parents involved but their involvement had continued throughout the time their child was in nursery and their commitment to their children's learning was sustained on transition into the infant school. Attrition, an acknowledged problem in many parent intervention programmes, was not a significant feature of this research and development project.

In the first year of the project much of the research and development work has been undertaken by the research team and a small core of the nursery staff, although all staff were involved in a practitioner research training programme. From 1998–2000 we wanted to encourage *all* staff to become more deeply engaged in the project so that much of the research work could become 'mainstreamed'. We wanted the key concepts training for parents, the sharing of information on children's development from home and from nursery to become part of the everyday activity of the community nursery. Only in this way could we be sure that these important activities could be sustained beyond the lifetime of the research project.

At various stages in the project staff needed to raise concerns over the increase in their workload as a result of the new ways of working. Sometimes they needed to discuss their anxieties when parents were hard to engage. It was also clear that certain staff were particularly excited by the project and it was important that they had 'time out' to become more actively involved. Other members of staff because of family commitments, pressures relating to other aspects of their work or personal inclination, were rather less engaged.

Having time to think and reflect on the work they do is critical if early childhood educators are to become increasingly rigorous and insightful in their practice. It is also important that the staff who work in the nursery know how to articulate their experiences (Drummond, 1989). When teachers do not have a clearly articulated pedagogical approach or a deep understanding of children's development then they may find it difficult to share information with parents and may perceive parents' questions as a challenge to their professionalism (Athey, 1990).

All nursery staff were allocated some additional time to make an extended home visit to interview the nursery child's parents, and to develop portfolios of the children's learning. Needless to say, the 'time out' allocation was never enough and was often at the end of an already very long day. When staff were involved in running study groups they were replaced in nursery. Towards the end of the project nursery staff who had also trained to work with adults were able to be paid to run the evening study groups through the local further education college.

All nursery staff were offered additional training in:

- video techniques;
- staff issues around being video recorded;
- ethical frameworks for interviewing;
- interview techniques;
- styles of engaging parents; and
- producing portfolios of children's learning.

The impact on staff

Members of the nursery staff who were asked to fill in questionnaires about what kind of an impact they felt the research project had made commented on the richer provision, the increasing in-depth nature of nursery planning sessions and the greater relevance of the experiences we were offering to children.

Angela, a senior family worker, reflected:

> I feel that the research project has given a focus to some parents and helped them to understand their children's learning and it has given us a opportunity to extend their learning. Parents have been able to discuss and challenge our teaching styles and our practice in an open and non-threatening way. The families in my group who have kept diaries have recorded many of their children's interests and this information was invaluable to me when I returned to work after maternity leave. I feel most parents who have been involved are able to talk about their child's learning positively and with confidence. I feel that the children have gained and that they are having their needs addressed and catered for.

Trevor Chandler, the Head of Centre, commented:

> Through attending the weekly research group, parents have shown their deepening level of understanding of their children's learning at home and the nursery. Through sharing this knowledge and experience in the group they have provided play and learning opportunities for their children based upon their child's dominant schemas. One mother who has a child with special needs described their holiday where her daughter experienced so many different sensory experiences. Her mother proudly celebrated her child's learning. The knowledge shared within the group has been regularly fed back to the nursery staff and informed the nursery's planning which, in turn, has enriched the child's experience.
>
> On the evening meetings, more fathers have been involved and they have felt included, and this has enriched their understanding of their child's play and learning opportunities. One father said that, following an evening meeting it has had a profound effect on his understanding of his child's play and behaviour, and he sees his son very differently now.

The perspective of early childhood educators and the research community

As a centre we are committed to supporting and training early childhood educators from the public, private and voluntary sector both locally and nationally. Staff at Pen Green were involved in training over 5,000 practitioners in 1999 (Bertram and Pascal, 2000).

Setting up a dissemination project for this work has become increasingly important as the project has developed. Both parents and staff from Pen Green have been involved in offering training to others. For example, local playgroups asked for and received training in child development concepts using the CD-ROM that the research team developed for use with parents. Local teachers in nursery classes in Corby have decided to set up small-scale projects, and staff and parents from Pen Green have worked alongside them.

What we have established at Pen Green is a multifaceted intervention project with, as its principal focus, parents' involvement in their children's learning. Small-scale projects like this one rarely have the staff time or funding to establish and maintain a database, and record the research process. At a cross-departmental review of provision for young children (1990) Marjorie Smith from the Thomas Coram Research Unit and John Bright from the Government's Social Exclusion Unit both made the point that it was essentially this kind of *process information* that was often not included in reports (Bright, 1998; Oliver, Smith and Barker, 1998). Yet this sort of information was of particular interest to organizations seeking to replicate good practice. This is why we decided to write up and publish the research and development project in an accessible format so that it could be used by a range of early years professionals. Through a series of national conferences and seminars other educators have also been offered training so that they can set up similar programmes in diverse locations. In February 2000 a new video was completed and this will form the basis for a new training programme which will hopefully support innovative and respectful work with parents throughout the UK.

Moving on

This research and development project has raised important issues for all of us. As we work hard to develop even more effective ways of working with children and parents we need to recognize:

- the great untapped energy and ability of parents and their deep commitment to supporting their children's development;
- the importance of developing a mutual understanding based on shared experiences;
- the need to have a clearly articulated pedagogical approach – when we are clear about our own beliefs then we can share them with parents;

- the need to employ staff who are confident, articulate, well trained and excited about working with adults as well as working with children;
- that it takes time to establish an equal, active and responsible partnership where parents decide what interests them; parents may write beautiful 'baby biographies' for a year at a time or just attend one session on understanding their children's educational needs. Parents need to get involved in their own time and in their own way;
- that working with adults in this way is always political. In Chris Pascal's (1996, p. 2) words, 'we want to encourage parents to stop accepting their lot and start creating the world they'd like to be part of'. In the words of Paulo Freire, it is about opening up for parents a 'language of possibilities' (Freire, 1970, p. 68).

3

Getting to Know the Families

Colette Tait

. . . our image of the child is rich in potential, strong, powerful, competent and, most of all, connected to adults and other children.

(Malaguzzi, 1993)

In this chapter I want to look at the many different ways we try to encourage parents to become involved in their children's learning. We have, over the last three years, developed a range of 'models of engagement' to appeal to as many different nursery parents as possible. Firstly, I will share how we 'get to know' the families we are working with, and want to appeal to. I will describe the nine different 'models of engagement' we have set up, how we monitor the uptake of the service by parents, some of the problems we have encountered and, finally, where involvement leads to for those parents who become deeply involved.

Family life in Corby

We recognize the fact that parents are not a homogeneous group – their lives vary greatly and, therefore, the 'method of engagement' that works for one family will not necessarily work for another. For us to be effective in engaging as many parents as possible we need to really 'get to know the families'. We also need to be prepared to adapt the ways we work in order to accommodate different families' needs, and also the continually changing needs of families. In one nursery year the changes listed in Table 3.1 were experienced by the families using the nursery.

Obviously, a family experiencing marital breakdown and access issues will have very different needs to a family who have just moved home.

Table 3.1　Major life events in the family

Event	Number reported	% sample
Change of job	16	32.7
Major illness	15	30.6
Change of address	12	24.4
Separation	12	24.4
Divorce	6	12.2
Someone moving out	6	12.2
Access difficulties	7	14.3
Someone moving in	10	20.4
Birth	9	18.4
Recent unemployment	9	18.4
Serious accident/illness	4	8.2
Other major events	9	18.4

Coping with transition

At Pen Green we have a community nursery and a playgroup (Educare) on the same site. Over the three years of the project we began to see increasing numbers of children 'sharing' places between the two provisions or combining a Pen Green nursery place with spending time with a childminder or a family carer. We suspected that children were having to cope with many different transitions on a weekly basis and so decided to find out where nursery children were spending their time each week. We asked parents to fill in a form (Figure 3.1, p. 38) telling us where their child spent time each week, including sleepovers because of shift work. This proved to be very useful data.

It is important that we are aware of the varying working patterns of the families who use the centre. Table 3.2 shows the many different shift patterns worked by some of our families.

Trying to be responsive

When children are allocated nursery places at Pen Green, they are also allocated a family worker. A family worker would have 8–10 children in his or her family group, and would aim to work and get to know the whole family, and not just the child attending nursery. Before the child even begins nursery the family worker would visit the family in their own home. The family worker would take with them a first visit/registration pack which gives the family some written informa-

Where and with whom does your child spend time on a regular weekly/fortnightly basis?						
Name of child						
Week I	a.m.	Lunch time	p.m.	tea time	Evening	Overnight
Monday Tuesday Wednesday Thursday Friday Saturday Sunday						

On an occasional basis my child may spend time with: (e.g., staying at friends, grandparents etc.)

It is really important for us to know where and with whom our nursery children spend time. For example, some children spend every other weekend with their father or grandparents, and it is important for us to listen and understand who they are telling us about and the experiences they are having.

Figure 3.1   Form to ascertain where a child spends time each week

tion about Pen Green. As well as form filling at this first visit, it is an ideal opportunity to start building up a good relationship with the whole family. During the nursery year the family workers continue to regularly 'home visit' their own families (Arnold, 1997b).

At the beginning of the research project we wanted to find out about family context, and the working patterns of both mothers and fathers. We set up a very basic database which would give us this information. This was done simply using a card index system.

Each card would show:

- the nursery child's name, date of birth, address and their family worker's name;
- the mother's name, address and working hours; and
- the father's name, address and working hours.

This, of course, presented problems immediately as many families did not easily fit into this template. What about those families where there had been a divorce or separation? What if either mother or father had a new partner . . . who do we try to engage? Should we concentrate

Table 3.2 Families' shift-work patterns.

Shift pattern		Factories
3-shift pattern:	6 a.m.–2 p.m. 2 p.m.–10 p.m. 10 p.m.–6 a.m.	Golden Wonder Weetabix
Continental shifts (including weekends) 4 days on, 2 days off 8 days on, 4 days off		Oxford University Press Quebecor
Twilight shift	5 p.m.–10 p.m.	RS Components Finnegans Famous Cakes
School hours	10 a.m.–3 p.m.	City Fax Asda
Part time	9 a.m.–2 p.m. 1 p.m.–6 p.m. 5 p.m.–10 p.m.	RS Components and many other local factories
Weekend shift	Friday nightshift and Saturday nightshift Saturday dayshift and Sunday dayshift	Solway Foods

our efforts on the child's biological mother or father, the child's step parent, everybody . . . or nobody?

Figure 3.2 is an example of the constitution of one family who currently use the centre. Once families separate, and become reconstituted families, it can become very complicated. Just who should we be sharing information with about the children's educational achievements and development? How do we define a family unit?

Parental responsibility: the Children Act definition

This was one of our first stumbling blocks. We decided to find out where we stood legally. We arranged for a local solicitor to come and hold a training session for staff about parental responsibility (PR) under the 1989 Children Act (Department of Health, 1991). We needed to know if by law, we were obligated to contact parents regarding

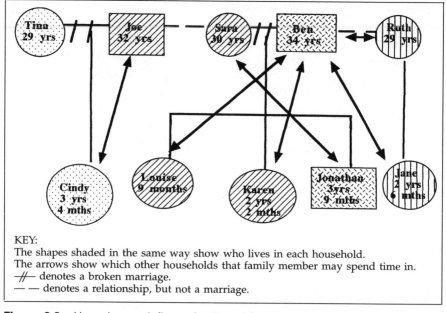

KEY:
The shapes shaded in the same way show who lives in each household.
The arrows show which other households that family member may spend time in.
─//─ denotes a broken marriage.
─ ─ denotes a relationship, but not a marriage.

Figure 3.2 How do we define a family unit?

their children; we also needed to know if there were situations in which it would be inappropriate for us to contact particular parents. We felt very strongly that parents needed to know 'the facts' about PR. This training session was incredibly informative and enlightening, and lots of different examples of family constitution were discussed. For example, one of our own nursery workers discovered that legally he did not have parental responsibility for his two children as he was not actually married to his children's mother, although he was their birth father. He had lived with his partner for 11 years and was named as the father on both the birth certificates. 'When I found out I didn't have parental responsibility I felt disrespected and unacknowledged. I have been a central figure in my children's lives' (Pen Green Family Worker).

Establishing PR was a much bigger issue than we had first anticipated. There were also added complications for the family workers – how would it be best to deal with the father who is known for his violent temper, and who we now realize does not actually have PR? There have also been instances in the past where mothers wanting to punish fathers have told centre staff that they are no longer allowed access to their child, and cannot for instance, collect their children from nursery when, in fact, they did still have PR. In these situations it was critical for us, as a staff group, to be clear about where we stood legally. We also realized that unless we were sure parents understood the relevance of PR then they would be likely to make the same assumptions that we, as a staff group, had made. For example, that if you are the biological father of a child you automatically have PR. We produced an information sheet for parents (Figure 3.3) telling them what parental responsibility was, who would automatically have PR, the consequences of not having PR, and, most importantly, how to obtain PR. Family workers then returned to families, armed

---

PARENTAL RESPONSIBILITY
Who has parental responsibility?
(Read this – it is not always who you think!)

Parental Responsibility is defined by the Children Act 1989. Not all parents have Parental Responsibility.

These people have parental responsibility:
1 The natural mother of the child.
2 The natural father of the child **provided he is married to the mother, or was married to her when the child was born subsequently**.
3 Anyone who has a Residence Order which is currently in force in respect of the child.

These people do not automatically have PR:
1 **The father of the child if he and the mother are not and have not been married.**
2 Grandparents or other relatives.
3 **Step-fathers**.
4 Guardians of the child appointed by Will.

What does this mean for my child in nursery?

• This means that at nursery consent forms can **only** be signed by parents with PR.
• That children can be collected by parents who do not have PR **but we must have written** consent from the parent who has PR.

How do I get Parental Responsibility?
Parental Responsibility can be acquired by formal **written** Agreement with the mother or by Order of Court. If you want to find out more many solicitors will offer a short consultation free of charge.

Figure 3.3   Parental responsibility information sheet

with this information, to clarify the situation.

We added to the card index system a note about who had PR for each individual child. We still, on occasion, have to call the solicitor to clarify a situation but, generally, all staff members and families using the centre are clearer about PR. This has made us more able to deal with difficult and sensitive situations, such as the biological father who does not realize he does not have PR.

So far, the database gave us some basic facts:

- who was in each household;
- the working hours of the adults; and
- which adults had PR.

What we then needed to do was make use of the database to monitor parents' involvement in the centre.

Using the database

We established this database early in the nursery year. We wanted to use it to find out how involved parents already were, and begin to look at ways of encouraging more families to become involved. We also wanted to develop other services or activities which might appeal to a wider range of parents. We needed to look at what was already happening within the centre and begin to build up a picture of the parents' involvement in their children's learning.

Building up a picture

When children start nursery at Pen Green there is a requirement that they are 'settled in' for the first two weeks. This means that either parent or an adult carer, perhaps a grandparent who does not have the same work commitments as many of our nursery parents, stays with the child in the nursery for this two week period. As well as enabling the child to become accustomed to nursery, this also gives the parent or carer a chance to see how the centre works and what other groups and activities are going on that they may be interested in. We noted, on our database, who settled each child in. Of course, this two-week period also enables family workers to get to know families more closely and begin to build a deeper relationship with the parents.

Once all the children are settled in nursery we hold four training sessions for parents on key child development concepts. These sessions are explained fully in Chapter 4.

These concepts underpin the practice in the nursery on a daily basis and help staff to look at how and what the children are learning. They help us to consider whether the nursery provision matches the interests of individual children. These key concepts have, over the last 5 or 6 years become 'tools' that help us to understand and develop our pedagogy. They help to increase our awareness about how children learn and communicate to parents and the wider community information about teaching and learning. Each of these training sessions is offered morning, afternoon and evening, with a free crèche, to accommodate the working patterns of our nursery parents. Again, we would monitor who attends the sessions and at what time of day.

At this point, reasonably early in the nursery year (October), we are beginning to build up a picture of the nursery families; we already know the working patterns of mothers and fathers. This enables us to hold groups or training sessions at times we know people are not working. We know whether adults in the nursery child's household have parental responsibility and we also know which parents have attended the key concept training sessions; but is this enough?

Parents' experience and aspirations

Although the database gave us basic information about each family's domestic constitution, it did not give us any information about the parents' own educational experiences or their aspirations for their children. Are our nursery children living with people who have had positive experiences of education themselves; do they have high expectations of their children . . . or not? We felt that we needed the answers to these types of questions, so we decided to produce a questionnaire. This questionnaire could be used as a guide during semi-structured interviews with parents. These would be interviews when we would hopefully find out the following kinds of information:

- at what age the parents left full-time education
- whether they had undertaken further education (FE) or higher education (HE);
- what they wanted for their child from the nursery; and
- what they believed their child was getting from the nursery.

As we wanted parents to feel comfortable and able to chat freely whilst taking part in these interviews we offered to do the interview either in their own homes, or in the centre. We found that, almost without exception, parents asked for the interview to be carried out in their own home. We assume from this that the nursery parents are comfortable with the staff, and the relationships generally appear to be strong and non-judgemental. The questionnaire was produced by members of staff and parents with the help of Dr Colin Fletcher, then Professor of Educational Research at the University of Wolverhampton.

We held two training sessions for staff who would be involved in carrying out these interviews. The training sessions looked at many issues. These ranged from staff's concerns about potential child protection issues that might arise during an interview, to worries about how long to allow for each interview. There were, of course, many concerns and anxieties expressed by staff members about their ability to carry out the interview. Maureen, one of Pen Green's Family Workers, recalls, 'initially I felt quite anxious about the interviews and therefore I really valued the training . . . when it came to carrying out the interviews I really enjoyed them and still do'.

Because of this quite a lot of time was allowed for staff to practise interviewing each other, in order to gain confidence. It was estimated that each interview would last approximately $1\frac{1}{2}$ hours. We also made the decision to buy in supply cover so that nursery staff were able to carry out their interviews without any added work pressure. Supply cover was 'bought in' for a series of whole days and half days. It was then up to each interviewer to contact his or her families and book themselves a time to carry out the interview, bearing in mind that only one member of the nursery staff could be released at any one time.

Mainstreaming the data collection

It became clear at a very early stage in the research project that the data we had collected was invaluable to the nursery staff. Three years on it is hard to remember how we managed without it. If early childhood settings are really committed to engaging all the parents using their services then it is essential information. Interviews have been carried out three times now – once a year over the last three years – and some quite significant changes have been made to the interview schedule and the interview process:

1   The questionnaire has been refined and shortened. Some of the questions on the original questionnaire have been added to the registration/first home visit pack, for example the question regarding parental responsibility. This is because we feel it is critical for nursery staff to have this information at the beginning of the nursery year. We have also removed some of the questions which did not elicit any relevant information.

2   One particular question has been removed from the questionnaire
    and is now carried out in family group meetings. This question
    was concerned with parents' attitudes to children displaying
    autonomous behaviour. We are particularly interested in this as
    our nursery is set up as a self-servicing workshop where children
    are encouraged to make decisions and to be masterful. We want
    our nursery children to become 'the manager of their own possi-
    bilities' (Laevers, 1995). This means that children as young as two
    are able to access materials with appropriate supervision and sup-
    port, such as real saws and hammers and scissors when they need
    them. In order to gauge parents' attitudes at the beginning of the
    nursery year we decided to show them, in a family group meet-
    ing, a short video clip of a young child using the workshop area
    in the nursery (Figure 3.4). Generally, once this has been shown a
    rich and varied discussion ensues in which all parents and staff
    present get to air their views. This has proved much more suc-
    cessful than asking parents to rate activities on paper. Perhaps this
    is because it is far easier for people who are not confident with
    writing things down to become engaged in a verbal debate.

3   A major change has been 'who carries out the interviews'. In the
    first year the interviews were carried out by family workers, the
    research team and the management team, but by the last year of
    the funded research project (1999) the family workers were very
    keen to carry out their own families interviews. This was almost
    a complete turnaround from the first year where the interviews
    were 'shared out fairly'. Family workers reported that, as well as
    being greatly enjoyable, the interview visits also helped them 'get
    to know' the interviewee's family more deeply. So, consequently,
    other members of staff only picked up on their interviews if
    absolutely necessary, for example, if a member of the nursery staff
    was on sick leave or maternity leave. This was a major piece of
    research and development work on the way to becoming main-
    streamed nursery practice! This was very important to us, as it
    was our ambition to mainstream the project. We wanted to ensure
    that it would be practical for the centre to continue the work
    beyond the lifetime of the funded project.

Using the interview information

Once all the semi-structured interviews were carried out we needed
to analyse the data. Each year we have worked with a researcher experienced in analysing interview data using SPSS (a statistical computer
package for social sciences). Initially the data analysis proved to be a

Figure 3.4 James in the nursery workshop area

very frustrating process for us. The questions we had found most interesting and which had helped to enhance relationships between workers and parents tended to be qualitative and, therefore, we were unable to analyse them using this package. We were, however, very aware that we had gathered information which we did not want to lose and so had to find ways to incorporate the qualitative data effectively into the reports we produced. One of the ways we did this was by including direct quotations. This tended to give a real 'flavour' of our nursery parents' home lives, their thoughts and their aspirations for their children.

The quantitative data

From the quantitative data gathered during these interviews we had a much clearer idea about the numbers of nursery parents who had themselves experienced schooling themselves as either a positive or negative experience. If parents have had negative experiences of schooling then they may find it hard even to enter the building. The centre is after all housed in the very school that many of our parents attended as children themselves. It is important, therefore, that staff are approachable and that the atmosphere is welcoming at all times. For example, we make a conscious effort to ensure that the rooms in which parents may attend groups or meetings are warm and comfortable. The chairs are usually arranged informally in a circle or semicircle, and there is always tea and coffee available for parents to help themselves to. To find out more about how we set up and run groups, please refer to Chapter 4.

One of the ways we try to 'make it OK' for parents to become involved; both in their children's learning and in the life of the centre, is by offering parents a range of different ways in which they can take part.

Models of engagement

I now want to describe some of the ways parents at Pen Green can become involved in their children's learning. We call these 'models of engagement'.

Attendance at initial key concept training sessions

As discussed earlier these sessions are run at the beginning of the nursery year and look at the four key concepts workers use which inform the work within the nursery. These groups are open to all parents/carers of nursery children. They run in the morning, afternoon and evening with a free crèche. It is critical that groups are run three times in one day, as the varying shift patterns some of our parents, work often prevent them from attending groups that happen, for example, only in the morning. If we only ran a group in the morning then some parents would only be able to attend the group every third or fourth week. The free crèche is also very important, as paying for childcare becomes prohibitive for parents on low incomes. This is sometimes a parent's 'first taster' of how groups are run at Pen Green.

Attendance at a long-term study group (Parents' Involvement in their Children's Learning)

Parent's have the opportunity to join a 'Parents Involvement in their Childrens Learning' (PICL) research group. Parents are able to attend this group the whole of the time their child is in the nursery. This group is described in detail in Chapter 7 but, briefly, this is a group which runs every week in the morning and afternoon for parents/carers to attend and discuss with nursery workers their child's development both at home and at nursery. Parents are given a diary and are encouraged to make notes during the week about what their children are doing. They usually describe what their children are doing when they are deeply involved in play or when they are displaying schematic behaviour. This, of course, raises issues about levels of literacy – would being given a diary alienate a parent with very low literacy levels? We also need to consider the families we work with for whom English is a second language. Through knowing our families, we can hopefully pre-empt either of these scenarios – perhaps the parents for whom literacy is an issue, or for whom English is a second language, could borrow the video camera, and bring a short video clip to the session – this is a method of information exchange that is always available to all families, whether they attend the research groups or not.

Family workers show short clips of video taken of the child playing in the nursery. This would be shown to the group and discussed in some detail.

Attendance at an evening PICL research group

This group runs in the same way as the weekly long-term study groups but was originally only run once a month for those parents unable to access the daytime groups. This group was initially set up to attract fathers – and advertised as a meeting rather than a group, which seemed to appeal to fathers. We now run this group on a weekly basis too, and have done so successfully for the past six months. One of the fathers who regularly attends the evening research group comments, 'I wouldn't miss a Thursday, they usually have a couple of minutes of video of him, and I like to see what he's getting up to'.

Individual sessions combining personal support, key concept training and information exchange

This model, again, appeals to a different set of parents. We feel that it is important to offer individual sessions for those parents who prefer to work in a one-to-one situation. Not all parents will enjoy being a part of a group – perhaps they perceive parents who attend groups as 'goody two shoes parents' and do not want to associate with them. Perhaps their life situation is currently overwhelming, and focusing directly on their child's development, without taking time to talk about their own issues, is impossible. This model of engagement gives the parent time to talk about themselves and their own family situation, as well as addressing the development of their child, both at home and at nursery (Shaw, 1991).

Home/nursery books

This is another very simple way of exchanging information with parents. A home/school book may include photos of the child in nursery with notes added by the family worker explaining what is happening in the photos. The family worker may ask for comments back from the parents about similar things the child is doing at home, and vice versa. This book is, of course, something the child can show to his or her grandparents, aunties and uncles, friends and is something for him to be proud of.

Home/school video

This is an ideal way for a working parent to become a 'fly on the wall' in their child's nursery (Epstein *et al.*, 1996). The family worker would video film a child in the nursery, and would perhaps add some comments themselves to the film to initiate a dialogue with the parents about the nursery child. This could then be sent home for the family to watch. As video cameras are used a lot in the nursery the children become accustomed to being filmed and see it as 'the norm'. There is also a video camera in the nursery that parents can borrow, so this can easily become a two-way exchange, with the nursery staff able to see the child playing at home. For example, when Chelsea's parents sent in some home video of Chelsea enveloping at home, the nursery staff were able to support and extend Chelsea's schema in the nursery, and support Chelsea with language about her activities at home.

Issue specific evenings

Parents are able to attend one-off events. These events may focus on, for instance, mathematics or technology and tend to be run as interactive workshops, so are quite a 'hands on' experience for parents. Interestingly these events have proven very popular with fathers/male carers. We need to find out whether this is because of the subject (for example, science and technology) or because they are 'one-off meetings' which have previously proven popular with male carers.

Trips to the Science Museum

Parents whose children are in their final year at nursery (some children attend the nursery for four to six terms) are offered the chance to go on a trip to the Science Museum. A group of parents, children and nursery workers would travel to London by train and spend the day at the museum particularly using the science discovery area. This has attracted many fathers and male carers who perhaps, in previous years, would not have become involved in their child's nursery life.

Family group meetings

Family group meetings are held each term; this has been custom and practice at Pen Green over many years. They are meetings run by each family worker to which all their nursery parents are invited. This is a chance for parents/carers to chat, not only to their family worker, but also to other parents whose children share the same family worker. When arranging a time for this meeting the family worker would look at the working patterns of his or her parents and would try to ensure the meeting was held at a time convenient to the greatest proportion of parents. These meetings tend to be very well attended and provide an opportunity for sharing information about the research project, chatting informally about child development and, again, reiterating the key concepts used on a daily basis in the nursery.

The range of models currently used to engage parents is clearly very varied, and, as well as these nine models of engagement, there are always informal chats when children are dropped off and picked up from nursery. There is always ample time for this as children are brought to nursery at any time from 8.15 a.m. – 10.00 a.m. There is no rigid start time. We are trying in this way to create space for as many parents as possible to become involved.

How do we know what's working?

It is all very well to offer all these different models but how do we know what's actually working? This is where we have to go back to the database.

As explained earlier, each time an event occurs (for example a family group meeting) a record would be taken of who attended and this would be recorded on the card index system. As well as recording attendance at events, we also noted down when home/school books or videos were exchanged. From this card index system we then set up a monitoring spreadsheet for each family group. This would be updated on a weekly basis, so that we could see at a glance who was accessing services and which services were proving most popular.

During the first year we carried out this monitoring exercise we realized, almost immediately, that there were not many fathers/male carers becoming directly involved. We decided that rather than second guessing the reason for this, the best thing to do would be to ask some of those men why they were not becoming involved.

It appeared, given the conversations we had, that the fathers we wanted to involve wanted a reason to come. All the fathers we spoke to said that of course they would attend their child's open evening once they were attending mainstream school 'because it's important for their education', but saw nursery as something different. The fathers did not want to 'share ideas about their child's learning' or have a chat and a coffee, which is the way in which we would generally advertise our groups. *These fathers wanted to know that they could make a difference to their child's education.*

Up until now, when we were advertising any groups or activities we would send a letter or poster home with whoever collected the child from nursery. We decided to send out two letters/posters per family – one we would mail directly to the father/male carer, providing he had PR, and the other would be handed to the person collecting the child from nursery – this person was generally the mother.

What we also decided to do was to differentiate between the posters which we wanted to appeal to mothers and those which would hopefully attract men/fathers. On posters for women we were generally more informal – inviting women to 'have a chat and a coffee' and 'share ideas'. On the posters for men we included more factual 'achievement-oriented' information, which would hopefully reflect more traditional male values (Marshall, 1994). For instance we included things like 'boys are under achieving – how you can make a difference'. Figure 3.5 offers one example of two posters advertising the same event.

This approach has been successful and we now always differentiate in the way that we advertise events and also always send information directly to those fathers who have parental responsibility.

Developing our understanding of parental involvement

During each year we have monitored the percentage of families of nursery children involved in some way. This has, of course, raised many questions for us, for example:

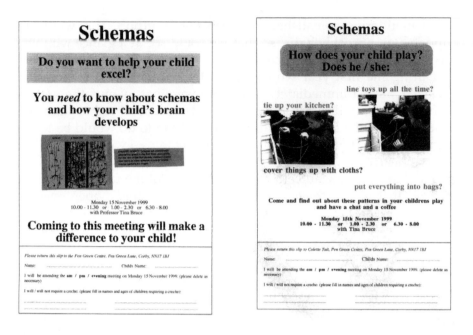

Figure 3.5 An example of two posters advertising the same event

- How do we define the nature of involvement?
- Do we distinguish between those parents who regularly attend one of the study groups and those parents who make use of a home/school book?
- What about those families we are still unable to engage?

We have used the same criteria each year whilst monitoring parental involvement in the project:

- Involvement, for us, is sustained use of any of the models of engagement. This would include the parent who, for example, only attends groups sporadically, but who keeps his or her diary on a regular basis, and discusses the child's learning with members of the nursery staff.
- We do not feel it would be very fair to distinguish between types of involvement – as we said earlier, not every method/model will suit every family. Even within one family one adult may come to a study group but the other adult may not be at all interested in that type of commitment. The other adult, however, may be very interested in technology and may enjoy sending and receiving videos of his or her child, or coming to issue specific evenings.

- We have struggled with the idea that there are some families we have not been able to engage. This has been a relatively small percentage, approximately 16 per cent each year (approximately nine families per nursery year).

Parents who do not get involved

With hindsight, we now think that we had an unreal expectation when the PICL research project began. We hoped that we would engage 100 per cent of families, and were concerned when we did not achieve this. We conjectured that the factors that might impinge on participation could be:

- marital status;
- the parents' employment;
- language barriers;
- family pressures;
- whether the child has one or two years in the nursery;
- whether the parent had a previous child in the nursery;
- parents' apparent hostility to any intervention;
- parents' education experiences;
- the family worker's (nursery nurse's) personality;
- changes in family life (e.g., sickness/pregnancy, etc.); and
- whether the child had special needs or there were other children in the home with special needs.

We returned once again to the interview schedules that we had carried out – it was apparent that many of the families were experiencing particular pressures and constraints. The emerging patterns that came out of the data were as follows:

- In two families both parents were working intensively to create a 'better' future for their children. In both cases, this involved a culture change, that is, sending their children to village schools outside Corby.
- In one family the father was working away as a long-distance lorry driver; in four families parents worked very anti-social shifts (one father was doing three jobs).
- Five out of nine of these other families had children who were only in the nursery for one year.
- Three out of nine of these families started nursery late and missed the critical two-week settling in the nursery period in September/October.
- Family pressures were very high in several families. These family

pressures included caring for a sick mother, three families with special needs children, two families living in violent houses, one where a mother had just got married, one family who had moved house and one family with a child with a severe health problem. In one family, both mother and father were learning disabled.
- In four families the nursery key worker changed during the year because of maternity leave or long term sick leave.

We have always been clear that parents need to get involved in their own time and their own way, but nevertheless we decided to discuss the issues of non-engagement with our advisory group. After lengthy debate we have realized that there are some families who do not wish to become deeply involved. If we have been responsive, flexible and persistent in offering these families different ways in and they still do not wish to be more involved, then we have to respect their wishes. We would, of course, continue to have informal chats with these carers, and share information about their children's learning in the nursery as well as ensuring all staff have access to ongoing training to enable them to work effectively with parents.

Staff's different strengths

As well as looking at numbers of families engaged (averaging 84 per cent each year) we have also looked at which model of engagement was most successful and which family worker had the greatest number of families involved in one way or another. This was not done in order to compare family workers pejoratively, but rather to identify training needs, individual strengths and to celebrate family workers' achievements.

This data analysis was very interesting; it appeared, each year, that if a family worker was directly involved in the research project, for example, perhaps as a leader of one of the study groups, then there were high levels of involvement from most of the parents in their family group in the research project. Whilst all family workers spend one nursery session per week out of the nursery and working with adults in a group situation, not all nursery staff are involved in running the research study groups. (The range of groups run at the centre varies greatly from toddlers' messy play sessions to therapeutic support groups). This was also backed up by the fact that the model of engagement which appealed consistently to the highest percentage of parents was the family group meetings.

From this we could assume that if a worker has a 'vested interest' in a certain project or meeting then he or she will be more effective in engaging families. Although we are sure that 'vested interest' is a significant factor in a family worker's effectiveness to engage parents, there have to be many other factors. For instance, some family workers' strengths may lie in one-to-one work. If this is the case, then they may not be enthusiastic about group work in the way that a worker who really enjoys working in groups will be and will therefore be less effective in 'selling' these groups to parents.

This has training implications for nursery staff that need to be addressed. Although some family workers are good 'all rounders', perhaps others would like to take up some specialized training. For instance, those members of staff who are very good in a one to one situation could go on and do counselling training, and those that enjoy group work could take up more advanced group work training.

Looking at levels of involvement in this way also showed, as expected, that the members of staff least experienced in working with adults were least effective in engaging families within the centre. Again this raises issues about staff training. We must ensure that all new members of staff are offered the same training opportunities as staff who have been at the centre for some time. It is important that training is reviewed annually.

The impact of 'getting involved'

For those parents who do become involved in their children's learning there are many benefits, relating to both their understanding of their children and their own raised self-esteem.

Over the last three years we have found that those parents who have been involved in their children's learning are keen to share their experiences with other parents. Louise comments 'After learning about schemas and Leuven Involvement I became a lot more tolerant . . . I began to understand why he was doing the things he was doing'. Louise and her family have obviously gained enormously through Louise's greater understanding of her son's development. Louise's husband, Scott, has recently become a school governor, and so will have a strong voice in his son's education in primary school.

Other parents appear to grow in confidence and feel more able to become advocates for their children. For example Lesley said 'I do feel more confident about going into Alice's school and asking questions'.

Many parents go on to deliver services, both within and outside the centre. As one father, Dave, commented: 'Due to my involvement with the PICL group I have been helping in the nursery on a voluntary basis. I have also been encouraged to pursue some formal qualifications in this field with a view to a career change in the future.'

Louise, who previously attended the nursery PICL group with her eldest son, who is now six, currently attends the PICL group to investigate her 3-year-old's learning. She also co-leads a Growing Together group for parents with children under three, 'I now co-run a PICL group called "Growing Together" which is aimed at 0–nursery age children and I find this very enjoyable and exciting – I love being able to share the experiences I had with my children with these parents, and also enjoying watching their children developing'.

Finally

Over the last three years we have learnt that we must try to:

- address staff training needs as they arise;
- ensure that there is gender differentiation, both in the way groups are run and advertised, and in the types of trips and outings offered to parents;
- work flexibly and responsively – giving parents what they want and need; and
- ensure that there are 'different ways in' for parents.

It is important to continually reflect on our practice, looking at what is working, and what is not, and responding accordingly. Happily, the project has affirmed our very strong belief that parents are committed to, interested in and excited by their children's learning.

4

Sharing Ideas with Parents about Key Child Development Concepts

Cath Arnold

This chapter considers ways in which parents can become involved in curriculum issues; describes the sorts of language and concepts the staff at Pen Green have been sharing with parents over a period of years; and looks at how to run group sessions and at what happens during those sessions.

Sharing ideas with parents

In 1990 Athey suggested that, 'Legislation cannot decree that parents and professionals should work together to increase knowledge of child development or to work out ways of how an offered curriculum might more effectively become a received curriculum' (Athey, 1990, p. 20). The notion of parents and professionals working together as equals on curriculum issues seemed a fairly radical idea when the Froebel Early Education Project was conceptualized during the early 1970s. The very idea that professionals do not have all the knowledge about the curriculum, which they can be ready to pass on to children and about which they can inform parents, was threatening to some professionals. For example, when my daughter started school in 1973, I was told on no account to allow her to do any writing at home as she was going to school to learn how to do it the teacher's way. Even though I was a knowledgeable parent, who had participated in some teacher training, I accepted that the school knew best. However, Chris Athey and her team demonstrated in the Froebel Early Education Project (1973–78) that when professionals share information about the curriculum, it is helpful to the parents, the children and their siblings (Athey, 1990).

Professionals also gain confidence from discussing and articulating their practice in an open way with parents. Athey says, 'the greatest benefit to teachers in working with parents is the spur towards making their own pedagogy more conscious and explicit' (1990, p. 66). It is this process of sharing ideas about child development theories and also listening to parents' detailed information about their own children that helps us to articulate our pedagogy more clearly. As professionals, we are sharing our specialized knowledge with parents and trying not to feel threatened by the fact that the parent will often see what is happening more quickly and clearly than we do. The recognition that the parents' specialized knowledge of their own child can stimulate our thinking is part of our professional development. Froebel Early Education Project has been an inspiration to the staff at Pen Green Centre and has greatly influenced our work with parents.

At the beginning of the twenty-first century, we have a government which is valuing the contribution of parents to their children's education. However, parents are still viewed by many practitioners as 'helpers' rather than as 'equal and active partners' (Whalley, 1997b) engaged in the process of education. Unless practitioners truly value the contribution made by parents, parents will continue to take on this less powerful role. If parents are listened to, then their children receive the powerful message that their family, its culture and values are worth something in the wider world.

What follows is an example of the sort of dialogue that is possible between workers and parents:

Example of a parent being involved in the curriculum at the Pen Green Nursery
For several weeks now, a small group of children and workers have been trying to make water-wheels to use in our new water run. The water is quite shallow at its source, so we have been experimenting with making our wheels work at the narrow trough towards the end of the run. One very simple idea we have been using is to push lolly sticks into some florist's oasis. Jack (aged 3½) is interested in objects that rotate. He has been involved in making and trying out various wheels. His family worker videos Jack involved in trying out the 'lolly stick and oasis' wheel and sends the tape home. Jack's mum, Donna, attends one of the weekly study groups, but we rarely see his dad, Tony, who works long hours. After watching the tape at home, Tony sends a message back to nursery, saying, 'Why don't you try attaching little paddles to the ends of the lolly sticks? That would help the wheel to turn more easily.'

Tony, the father in this example, had obviously looked closely at the video and felt able to offer an idea about how to extend and improve our experiment. Although we rarely see Tony, we are involved in solving a problem together, which contributes to the curriculum we are offering the children (including Jack) at nursery.

Practitioners are looking for practical ways forward. Many parents are waiting to be invited to participate.

Ways of becoming involved

Since parents are not a homogeneous group they all have different needs and different starting points. They will want to get involved in their children's early years settings in very different ways.

(Whalley, 1997b, p. 17)

We have just heard how Tony is becoming involved in Jack's education at nursery. Tony has already been present for a home visit from Jack's family worker. He has also attended an open evening at the nursery. For the open evening, the nursery was set up for parents and children to explore what is available each day and to chat informally with workers. What the example in the last section illustrates is a dialogue between practitioners and parents about curriculum issues.

Parents are currently involved in their children's education at Pen Green in the following ways:

- through daily chats with their child's family worker and other nursery staff;
- by attending sessions about key child development concepts (these sessions will be fully explored later in this chapter);
- by attending a nursery open evening;
- by keeping a diary of what their children do at home;
- by borrowing a nursery video camera to film their child at home;
- by receiving some video of their child filmed at nursery (like Jack's family);
- by attending a weekly study group during the day;
- by attending a weekly study group in the evening;
- by attending a family group meeting;
- by going on a trip to the Science Museum in London with their own child, two members of staff and other parents with their children
- by attending issue specific workshops, e,g., science and technology;
- by attending individual sessions; and
- by contributing to a home/school book.

Sharing a language about the curriculum

In Chapter 2 we talked about the need for an honest exchange of ideas with parents using a shared language. Any field of knowledge has its own language or jargon. A specialist language may be a barrier to communicating with parents. If we want power to be shared with parents, then the first step is to share any specialized language we are using. At Pen Green we have been exchanging information with parents about 'schemas' or 'patterns of behaviour' for about ten years now (Athey, 1990; Bruce, 1997). Parents usually pick up this technical language very quickly and apply it to what their own children are doing. We have numerous examples of parents understanding and using 'schematic language'. For example,

> Sean's dad (about Sean's arrangement of his cars): 'Youse would call it infilling.' Sean's mum (about Sean throwing a piece of lego, which hits Margy's head): 'He's targetting a trajectory.'

> Matthew's mum (about Matthew): 'It's all become so clear, just like curtains opening – now I know he's into trajectories, I can understand him much better.' (And Matthew's sister, Amy): 'She's a transporter – I find different ways that she can carry things to nursery – a sling for her doll, a bike for her to ride on.'

> William's mum (about William): 'He envelops his cars and trains with mud, then puts them under running water and washes the mud off.'

> Levie's mum (about Levie): 'She likes transporting books – she irons them with her toy iron.'

When we share this technical language with parents, we also share our knowledge about how their children learn. It gives us a clear focus. So, as workers, rather than just saying to a parent, 'William has had a lovely time playing today' (which, in fact, tells them very little about what William has actually been doing at nursery), we can say, 'William really enjoyed building a vertical trajectory with hollow blocks today' (a more specific statement about what William has actually been doing).

We could choose to simplify our language but parents might find that patronizing. We can hardly claim a wish to be equal partners if we arbitrarily decide that the language is too difficult for parents to understand. Of course, we might explain that it was a 'very tall tower' and that William called it 'Notre Dame'.

As soon as we begin to share language about the curriculum,

usually on the initial home visit, we are making our pedagogy more explicit (Drummond, 1993). Each explanation we offer, helps us to understand the concepts more fully.

An example of making pedagogy more explicit

After working in the nursery for four months, Michele volunteered to show some students around. She was nervous at first but found that she enjoyed explaining about how individual children learn through 'schemas' or 'patterns of behaviour'. After the students' visit, Michele realized that, in helping the students to understand children she knew well, she had gained a greater understanding of how children learn and also that she felt a little more confident about her knowledge of schemas.

Although the dialogue with parents begins with the initial home visit (before a child starts nursery) and continues throughout each child's time at nursery, we do not expect parents just to pick up ideas in a haphazard way. We plan and devote time to giving every parent the opportunity to learn about the key child development concepts we are using in the nursery. Some of these key concepts were described in Chapter 2. There are four concepts that we find particularly helpful:

- involvement (Laevers, 1994a, 1997);
- well-being (Laevers, 1997);
- adult style (Rogers, 1983; Pascal and Bertram, 1997; Whalley and Arnold, 1997a); and
- schemas (Athey, 1990; Bruce, 1997).

Using a groupwork model to share ideas with parents

Early childhood educators are in the unique position of coming into contact with children and their parents or carers on a daily basis. Because of this daily contact and a shared interest in the children, they are well placed to work with those adults as well as with their children. However, initial training, whether it is National Nursery Examination Board (NNEB), NVQ or teacher training, does not usually prepare early educators for working with adults. Therefore, workers do need to undertake some groupwork training. This kind of training is offered to all staff at Pen Green on a regular basis.

When planning the curriculum for young children, educators using a constructivist approach consider what each child brings to the learning situation (Athey, 1990, p. 43). In a similar way, we need to consider the rich experiences that adults bring to any learning situation and to adopt a 'person centred' approach to adult education (Whitaker, 1986, p. 277). Whitaker says, 'Experience of small group work had led me to the belief in the power of groups to provide a particularly rich and creative learning environment for human growth' (ibid., p. 276). He goes on to describe ways in which adults can 'share and draw on the considerable knowledge, experience and expertise present in the group' (ibid., p. 278).

The Open University course team, in its notes to group leaders, refers to 'learner-centred study groups' (Whalley, 1996b, p. 7): 'This way of working acknowledges the fact that adult learners are not simply empty vessels waiting passively to be filled; they are highly motivated mature learners who bring an enormous amount of life experiences to each study group.' The study groups we have set up at Pen Green, as part of the Parents' Involvement in their Children's Learning project, are discussion groups during which parents 'compare notes with nursery staff and watch video tapes of their children playing in nursery and at home' (Whalley, 1997b, p. 17). We are trying to create an environment in which 'adults reflect on their own past experiences, relate their present to their past experiences and access new information' (Whalley, 1996b, p. 7). Within this type of environment there are 'tangible gains' for the leaders as well as for the group members.

Creating an environment and planning a session

There are several important practical issues to consider when we are planning to run sessions for parents on key concepts.

Timing

Parents are most keen to know about their children's development when the children have just started nursery (Arnold, 1997a). Therefore, it is crucial to arrange to run our training sessions during the first month or six weeks. These initial sessions are an important foundation on which to base our ongoing dialogue with the parents.

Time of day is also important. In order to give each parent an opportunity to attend each session, we run each session three times a day, that is, morning, afternoon or evening. (Parents have been known to attend more than one session on schemas in a day, they found it so enlightening they came back for more!)

Crèche

We always offer parents a crèche for their children. This enables them to participate in the sessions without distractions. We are also flexible about having children in with us during the sessions if they do not settle in crèche. (One little boy, James, clearly revealed his strong 'rotation' schema during an evening session in which we were using the carousel projector. He peered at the projector from every angle and was mesmerized by it each time it moved. This, along with the information his mum shared with the group about his interests at home, confirmed his strong interest in 'rotation').

Invitations to attend

We send out two invitations, one to the child's mother and one to the child's father. Word of mouth is important, because parents usually want to know more than is on the initial letter or poster. This also helps us to make sure we include everyone, whatever their level of literacy. Each family worker talks to the parents of the children in their family group about the sessions. We might also have a large poster in the nursery so that parents can sign up and book crèche facilities.

Setting up the room

Comfortable armchairs arranged in a circle help parents to relax. (If armchairs are not available, then adult-sized chairs would do). We try to make the room more like a living room than a classroom. It is important to have tea and coffee available and to make drinks for parents as they arrive.

Planning the sessions

We have found that groups run more smoothly if two workers run each session. The content delivery needs to be planned well in advance. However detailed and meticulous the planning, it is very important to be flexible and to allow plenty of time for parents to express their views. This is often the first time the parents have returned to an 'educational environment' since they left school and strong feelings about school often emerge in the group. Although parents may themselves have had poor experience of the education system, most are clear that they want their children to succeed. If, as workers, we do not allow parents to express their views freely, then they may continue to experience the system as letting them down in some way. This is particularly relevant in Corby, where very few adults have experienced further or higher education.

The group leaders can consider in advance what is likely to happen during the initial meeting of the group. Like any small group, to be effective, the group has to work on at least two levels:

- group task – tackling the business of the group; and
- group process – satisfying social needs and meeting people's needs for acceptance, recognition, belonging etc. (Whalley, 1996b, p. 11).

Training in groupwork prepares us to think about what to do if a group member completely dominates the session or seems not to participate at all. The two workers can agree beforehand to take on different roles during the session. One can lead and try to keep the group on task, while the other can support individual parents and make sure that quieter parents are heard. Rather than the two workers sitting together, it can be more enabling for group members if the two leaders are part of the group. Sitting alongside a parent, who might be vulnerable, is a helpful strategy.

However well we have planned the content of the group in advance, each group takes on a dynamic of its own which no one can anticipate. This makes each session exciting and interesting for everyone involved.

A typical session

Each of the initial key concept sessions would begin with one of the group leaders introducing herself and trying to put parents at their ease. Humour might be appropriate, for example, if everything has gone wrong for the leader that day, she might share that with the group. If anyone in the room is worried about leaving their child in the crèche they will be offered reassurance. Children are always brought back to parents within five minutes if they do not settle. This sets the tone for the group. The leaders can demonstrate that whatever is important to the group members is important to the whole group.

She would then ask each parent to introduce themselves to the rest of the group and perhaps say something about their own child. Occasionally a parent is reluctant to do this and we must accept their decision. If they agree to introduce themselves, then the ice is broken and they have spoken in the group for the first time. People can get quite anxious waiting for their turn.

For these initial key concept sessions, we try to engage as many parents as possible. The study groups work best with eight to ten members and this is borne out by the research. According to Mullins (1989, p. 376) 'cohesiveness becomes more difficult to achieve when a group exceeds 10–12 members'. If the group is larger than the optimum number, then it works better to ask each person to move around the room and introduce themselves individually to other group members. This is less threatening and can be fun, but may take longer.

During each session, one of the group leaders introduces the theory underpinning the concept to be covered in that session.

Session 1: Involvement

This session would begin with a brief introduction to the work of Professor Ferre Laevers and the theory underpinning the concept of 'involvement'. Laevers's work is well established and rigorous, and it is particularly accessible to early years' workers. We have found that parents readily take on these ideas.

The important point to convey to parents is that Laevers has been looking at the processes of learning as well as the outcomes or products. He is interested in what is happening inside each child as they learn. He has developed a scale and signals to describe how 'involved' each child is in what they are doing at any given moment (Laevers, 1997). Being deeply involved means that a child is developing and learning, and that fundamental changes are occurring.

At that point in the session, we would show some of our own nursery video of a child deeply involved. A favourite clip of ours is Lynsey mixing pasta, water and other materials at a table. As she moves her arm across the table, she knocks a metal pan to the floor, it clatters but she is not distracted from what she is doing. We would ask the parents to discuss Lynsey's level of involvement. We would contrast that clip with a piece of video where a child is less involved, for example, when an adult is taking too strong a lead and not noticing what the child is really wanting to do. Some discussion of the concept of 'involvement' would follow. This is often when parents begin to relate their experiences of their own child to more general child development theory.

Next we would hand out sheets outlining signals and levels of involvement. Laevers (1997, p. 19) says,

> We speak about involvement when children (or adults) are intensely engaged in an activity. They are in a special state. They are concentrating and are eager to continue with the activity. They feel intrinsically motivated to carry on, because the activity falls in with what they want to learn and know ...

The signs of involvement Laevers has identified are:

- concentration;
- energy;
- complexity and creativity;
- facial expression and composure;

- persistence;
- precision;
- reaction time;
- verbal expression;
- satisfaction (ibid., pp. 20–1).

Not all the signals would necessarily be present at once, though four or five of the signals are usually apparent when a child (or adult) is deeply involved. The signals are considered alongside 'a continuum ranging from "no activity at all" (level 1) to "total implication in the activity" (level 5)' (Laevers, 1994b, p. 163). Further discussion with the parents would then follow. We emphasize the point that when we are rating a child's involvement, we are not judging the child but we are judging the provision we offer them at nursery.

An example of providing for a child's needs and using his involvement as a gauge
When Geoffrey started nursery he appeared to 'flit' from one area to another and was constantly 'on the move'. After observing him closely, we realized that he spent a great deal of his time 'checking out' what was on offer in each area of the nursery. He was rarely judged to be 'deeply involved'. We noticed, however, that he spent up to five minutes and displayed some of the signals of involvement when playing in the sand. We used this information to collect resources and to set up a 'site office', for example, hard hats, vehicles, sand, gravel, spades, guttering, mobile phone, clipboard, tape measure and spirit level. We took Geoffrey and other children on a visit to a building site. Subsequently, Geoffrey began to play for longer periods of time and to become involved in more complex play, for example, role-playing 'being a builder'. Eventually, he began to co-operate with other children and to extend his sustained play to other areas of the nursery.

We point out that when a child is deeply involved (that is at level 4–5) they are really developing and learning. This is the perfect time to observe a child and to capture on video or to write down what they are doing. If a child is deeply involved then the learning experience is obviously important to the child and therefore gives us a clue as to what to offer them next. Involvement comes in peaks and troughs. Each child has his or her own rhythm (Arnold, 1997a). Whilst we would not expect children or adults to be deeply involved all the time, if we never see children deeply involved, then we must look at how we are supporting their learning. Children do need to be challenged. 'Involvement only occurs somewhere between "being able to do something" and "not yet being able to do something"; "under-

standing something" and "being on the verge of understanding" '
(Laevers, 1997, p. 20).

If there is time towards the end of the session, the group would
practise rating levels of involvement using short video clips. This
could be individually or in pairs. As a group, we could think about
what we, as adults, become deeply involved in. If we can empathize
with children, then that helps us to understand and to encourage the
children in what is important to them.

Session 2: Well-being

Introductions are an important beginning to all of the sessions.
Sometimes the group will consist of the same people and at other
times new people may arrive. Some parents work shifts and have to
attend sessions at different times of day and so join different groups
each week. Beginning in the same way each time establishes a kind
of format, and the predictability of using a similar format is com-
forting for some parents and workers. It may be that a parent who
refused point blank to say anything during the first session, feels more
confident when they come to the second session purely because they
know the sorts of things other people say.

After the introductions, we would ask parents to think back to their
own childhoods and to think about a time or times when they were
happy. After a few minutes' reflecting on this, we would ask each
member of the group to share their memories with the person next
to them. As workers, we would participate in this exercise, being sensitive to particularly shy parents or to parents who may feel left out.
If a parent was new to the Pen Green Centre or had a special need,
the workers would watch, and see whether another parent made a
move to include this new parent. If no other parent included the new
parent, usually because there is an odd number of people in the
group, then one of the workers would pair with him or her. When
the talking dies down (usually after ten minutes or so), we would ask
people to share their memories with the large group. We are always
clear that there is no requirement to share these memories with the
large group. For some people, this exercise can be distressing. One
parent, for example, could remember no happy times during her
childhood.

Using ideas generated in the group, we would jot down some key
words on a flipchart. Examples are 'holidays', 'the fair', 'playing out
with my friends', 'playing shops on my own'. (Sadly, few people men-
tion school.) After sharing memories of the experiences, we would try
to remember and identify the feelings associated with those experi-

ences. Examples are 'excitement', 'being in charge', 'exhilaration', 'contentment'.

When the group have explored their own ideas about feelings associated with happy times, one of the workers would introduce the work that Laevers has been carrying out on children's emotional 'well-being' (Laevers, 1997, p. 17). The workers at Pen Green have met Laevers and have been impressed with his value base. We have found that his theory of the concept of 'well-being' is one on which we can operate. The emotional well-being of their children is always a concern of parents and carers, especially when children are starting to attend nursery or any new setting.

Laevers is interested in what is going on inside children while they are learning. Many factors can stop children from being able to learn. The way that Laevers describes the inability to learn is through each child's 'level of well-being' (Laevers, 1997:15). He says that 'the level of well-being in children indicates how they are doing emotionally' (ibid.). Once again, we are looking at how well we, in the nursery, are meeting the needs of individual children. 'The degree of well-being shows us how much the educational environment succeeds in helping the child to feel at home, to be her/himself, to remain in contact with her/himself and have her/his emotional needs (the need for attention, recognition, competence . . .) fulfilled' (Laevers, 1994b, p. 5). Laevers comments that 'crying is not necessarily an indication of low well-being' (Laevers, 1995). Crying may mean that a child is in touch with their own feelings.

Laevers has identified 'a number of characteristics in a child's behaviour' to which we might refer in order to assess each child's well-being. Not all of the characteristics need to be present for a child to be at a high level of well-being. At least half of the signals being present indicate a high level of well-being. These are the signals:

- openness and receptivity;
- flexibility;
- self-confidence and self-esteem;
- being able to defend oneself and self-esteem;
- vitality;
- relaxation and inner peace;
- enjoyment without restraints; and
- being in close contact with one's inner self (Laevers, 1997, pp. 18–19).

Some of the signals link closely with our own work on 'Learning to be Strong: assertiveness for under-fives'. Whalley (1994, p. 78) says,

'Our concern with children's emotional needs also led us to watch the withdrawn, vulnerable children in the nursery more carefully. We became more and more aware that these children had few strategies for coping with anger or hostility from their peers'.

In 1986, we began working with children in small groups and using role-play to explore ideas about friendships, bullying, boundaries, strangers and feelings. Now we routinely offer children an opportunity to express their feelings and fears, to learn some new strategies and to practise using these strategies in a safe environment with the support of adults.

At this point in the key concept session we would give parents a hand out listing Laevers's signals for well-being. We would go through and discuss each one in more detail and compare them with the feelings the group had identified that day. We hope that parents will discuss well-being in relation to their own children. Again, this can be a tricky issue. It is often easier for a parent to reflect on the fact that their child's well-being was low two months ago because the dog died, than it is to talk about a child whose well-being is low today because of a family row.

We hope that we are giving parents permission to express their feelings about their children or about themselves. We are certainly saying that each child's emotional well-being is the foundation on which their education is built.

We would discuss strategies for helping young children to express their feelings. We have a good selection of storybooks in the nursery, that deal with a range of feelings and we would suggest suitable stories which parents might then use. A parent mentioned that her child was scared that Santa Claus would come into her bedroom. *Worried Arthur* by Joan Stimson (1995) deals with this issue and even describes a strategy, that is, leaving Santa a note saying, 'Please if it is at all possible, as my bedroom is a little untidy . . . could you leave any presents just here'. This parent borrowed the book to read to her child and found it very helpful.

This session might also alert us to the fact that a parent has painful feelings that are unresolved. We can acknowledge this afterwards with the parent and make sure that this parent knows that professional help is available. We can recommend organizations or individual counsellors if the parent is ready to seek help.

Session 3: Adult style

After the introductions, one of the group workers introduces the idea that the engagement style adopted by adults affects how children learn. We begin by introducing the descriptions of adult style used in the Effective Early Learning Project at University College Worcester (Pascal and Bertram, 1997).

Rogers drew attention to the 'facilitative attitudes' of some therapists as perceived by their clients: 'When clients in therapy perceived their therapists as rating high in genuineness, prizing and empathetic understanding, self-learning and therapeutic change were facilitated' (Rogers, 1983, p. 128).

The facilitative styles adopted by the Effective Early Learning Project are

- stimulation;
- sensitivity; and
- autonomy.

We would offer brief descriptions, then watch some of our own video clips and discuss the styles being used by different educators. Extremes are useful in order to illustrate the differences in style of individual members of staff. We have one clip, filmed on a visit to a European nursery, where an adult leans over a child from behind the child and places the child's hands on its collage. It is obvious that the child has very little autonomy. One father compared this with his experience at Corby Police Station when he was arrested and had his fingerprints taken! We have generally found it less threatening to discuss the styles of people we do not know or are never likely to meet.

Another clip shows one of our own workers working in the block area with two 2-year-olds. She works at the children's level (physically) and moves between the three styles with amazing skill, encouraging the two children to co-operate in some shared building, keeping them safe while encouraging them to move to the edge of their capabilities. The children's involvement in this joint venture is sustained for 20 minutes.

Usually there is a great deal of discussion and sometimes disagreement about what individuals think is happening in the video clips. A wide range of opinions are usually expressed about autonomy. One parent recently commented that, 'I can understand you not allowing children to operate technical equipment like videos in nursery because of the younger children, but Chloe operates the video on her own all of the time at home'. Sometimes children are allowed more autonomy at nursery than at home, for example, when using real tools, but in this instance Chloe is allowed to operate the video at home but not at nursery.

During the session on adult style, we would also give the parents a handout describing our own work on adult pedagogic strategies (these are discussed in full in Chapter 5). After sharing and discussing the pedagogic strategies, we would watch some more video clips and try to analyse them in terms of the eight strategies that staff and parents at Pen Green have identified. This might stimulate more discussion about, for example, 'what is appropriate risk?' or 'how can we help children go beyond our own knowledge base?'

Session 4: Schemas

Our session on schemas is slightly different as we usually invite Tina Bruce, an early years consultant and professor at the University of North London, to introduce the idea of schemas to parents. She is always supported by a member of our nursery staff. Tina Bruce was the teacher in the original Froebel Early Education Project and has worked as a pedagogic consultant to Pen Green for many years. The introductions in this session are very important as Tina is not based at the centre and generally does not know all of the children.

After the introductions, Tina usually uses a flipchart to begin to illustrate and describe the basic schemas. She talks about up/down movements (*vertical trajectories*), side-to-side movements (*horizontal trajectories*) and slopes (*oblique trajectories*). Tina offers the colloquial or everyday language and also the schematic language to describe each schema or pattern (Athey, 1990). She would then move on to *enclosures and rotation*.

Tina would then begin showing slides to illustrate each of the common schemas. She would talk us through the surrounding context including the emotional needs of children she is describing. Tina encourages the parents to chip in and talk about their own children. The role of the nursery worker in this session is to make links between what children have been doing in nursery and any schemas Tina is illustrating. Tina works in this way so that there is some 'power sharing' during the session (Whalley, 1996b, p. 25). She is trying to engage the parents in discussion, and the more lively the session the more engaged the parents are in grappling with the ideas. The discussion continues throughout the session and usually some parents express their amazement at having a new understanding of their child's actions for perhaps the first time.

Working with the sceptics

Occasionally, parents will express the view that it is 'a load of tosh'.

Even these sceptical parents can become intrigued or interested after watching or videoing their own children at home. Sometimes parents will come back when a second or third child starts attending nursery. At this point, with more time to watch their child, they begin to understand the significance of schemas.

Parents are always given *A Schema Booklet for Parents* (Mairs, 1990) on their initial home visit. They can use this to refer to initially and they often ask for more information on schemas. We would recommend various booklets and articles and we would also say,

- watch your child;
- talk to your Family Worker; and
- attend one of the study groups.

We invite parents both to attend and to speak at conferences held at the Pen Green Centre. By talking about their own children to a wide range of workers, the parents contribute a great deal to current knowledge about young children. Nothing is more impressive than hearing a parent speak with passion and confidence about their own child. The experience of speaking to an audience of 150–200 people can have a huge impact not only on the audience, but on the parents themselves and on other parents who use the Centre.

Although there is some direct teaching of theory during each session, the emphasis is on involving each member of the group in discussion. It is helpful to acknowledge that people learn in different ways (Gardner, 1983; Dryden and Vos, 1994; Whalley, 1999a). Each session contains some auditory information and some information that is presented visually; however, most information is shared through interpersonal discussion. There is usually a written handout. Whenever possible, participants draw on their own firsthand experiences or observations. We are trying to involve the participants in whichever way suits them best. If parents are too shy to contribute to the group discussion, we can offer them an individual session at another time.

Sustaining interest in the key concepts

The sessions introducing key concepts to parents described in this chapter, are only part of the story. It is not simply a case of sharing the concepts with the parents, who then go away with a full understanding, able to operate on them effectively. Unless the parents become involved in discussing and making use of these concepts, they will have very little impact. However, if a parent takes a diary and we suggest that they write down what their child does when they are 'deeply involved' (Laevers, 1997), this leads to further discussion and analysis. The concepts are not something we add on or use as a tokenistic salute to theory. They are very useful concepts that help us to understand and to discuss children's development and learning with parents and colleagues on a daily basis.

One way we have 'managed' to hold those daily conversations with parents is to target one or two children for observation each day. We have then targeted these children's parents or carers at the end of the session, so that we are also gathering information about what the children are currently doing at home. We have found that these conversations help to enrich our summative assessment of each child's development and learning. Parents' evenings are much more relevant when they are continuations of a dialogue engaged in during the school or nursery year.

Many of us are are struggling with record-keeping, and we can lighten our load by involving parents. 'Working with parents' makes our workload more manageable. Parents are definitely interested – they are only waiting for an invitation from us.

A very real constraint for all early childhood settings is lack of money and resources. Conversation is valuable and costs us only the effort. Notebooks can be bought for about 10 pence each and that is all that parents need to start keeping a diary. We are finding that each child's record of nursery or school is much more relevant when it includes information from their parents.

When sharing ideas with parents in this way we find it is important to remember that:

- parents are experts on the subject of their own children and can share their expertise with professionals;
- it can be helpful if professionals share specialized language and concepts with parents;
- professionals can use a groupwork model to share information with parents about key child development concepts; and
- practitioners need to be open and honest with parents and to see them as allies in collecting information about children's development and learning.

5

Parents and Staff as Co-educators – 'Parents' Means Fathers too

Margy Whalley and Trevor Chandler

This chapter explores the importance of the adult role in supporting and extending children's learning within early years settings. Parents and early years professionals need to work closely together if we are to provide the optimum opportunities for children to learn and develop. 'Parents and teachers can help children separately or they can work together to the greater benefit of the children' (Athey, 1990, p. 66). We have used two pieces of action research to highlight the importance of recognizing mothers' and fathers' role as their children's first and most consistent educators.

Parents and staff as co-educators

The approach that we use in working with parents is rooted in the philosophy and ethos of our centre. Traditionally, parent education programmes have been based on a deficit model, targeting the families perceived to be most in need. For example workers in the Headstart programme in the USA assumed that 'parents would benefit from the intervention of professionals, organised the relationship on professionals' terms, and tended to see children as needing to be rescued from inadequate backgrounds' (Ball, 1994, p. 44). Pugh and De'ath critique this kind of approach as 'programmes that rely on professionalism disempower parents'. (Pugh, De'ath and Smith, 1994, p. 88). In Chapter 1 we describe the community development approach to working with parents and it is this way of working that underpins our approach to developing a deeper understanding of the adult's role in extending children's learning.

Constructivists: interactionists

The importance of the adult in supporting and extending children's

74

learning is well documented. The way in which the adult supports the child depends upon the adult's belief in how children learn. As early years workers, the relationship between the professional and the parent or carer is also influenced by our beliefs about what working together in partnership really means. Malaguzzi, the philosopher and pedagogue who worked in partnership with parents and educators in Reggio Emilia, describes this process as

> 'understanding the child as a co-constructor, an active participant, wanting and responding to a wide range of relationships, in the home and outside, with other children and adults . . . We can open up the possibility of a childhood of many relationships and opportunities, in which both the home and the early childhood institution have important, complementary but different parts to play.'
>
> (Malaguzzi, cited in Dahlberg, Moss and Pence, 1999, p. 52)

The timing and level of intervention by the adult is crucial in helping or hindering a child's learning. To require children to work within an adult-imposed framework is not helpful. If what is being offered to the child bears no relation to the child's own interests then children will not become deeply engaged. On the other hand, if children are left to 'just get on with it' they may become frustrated. It seems that the natural instinct of many adults is to do things for children, especially if they are in a hurry or if they cannot bear to see the child struggling.

At Pen Green we subscribed to a constructivist approach. Athey describes constructivists as 'child-centred teachers who are trying to become more conscious and more theoretically aware of what is involved in the process of "coming to know". Constructivists are interested in the processes by which children construct their own knowledge' (Athey, 1990, p. 30). Bruce (1997, p. 10) calls this way of working an interactionist approach. It seemed to us that parents and staff needed to share their understanding of this way of working. We needed to know more about the strategies that parents and nursery staff adopt when interacting with children in the home setting and the nursery setting. We wanted to look more closely at the ways in which all the important adults in children's lives support their learning and development so that we could identify strengths and avoid inconsistencies in our various approaches.

Adult engagement styles

In Chapter 4 we describe the concept of the adult engagement style and describe how this concept is shared with parents. It was from the start a far more problematic concept for parents and staff than involvement, well-being and schemas. Pascal and Bertram (1997) use three main descriptors to describe the adult styles of engagement:

- autonomy;
- sensitivity; and
- stimulation.

Nursery staff and parents struggled with these definitions and examples when we first encountered them through the Effective Early Learning project (EEL) (Pascal and Bertram, 1997). We were well aware that the adult's ability to engage the child was a critical factor in terms of the child's ability to become deeply involved in learning. However, we found it hard to achieve any consensus as to the degree of autonomy that was optimal to children's learning or what behaviour on the part of the adult constituted 'sensitive engagement'. Some of the nursery staff had experienced using the EEL measures with groups of teachers and had found that, even in professional groups, it was often difficult to achieve a consensus on the basis of these classifications. Early years practitioners tended, in the first instance, to make judgements from their own value base (Drummond, 1993). During the training programmes that are a core part of the EEL project, early childhood educators are given time and training to work through these issues so that the judgements they make are moderated against those of others.

When we watched videos of adults providing stimulating 'materials' for children it often seemed to us that the interventions were too adult directed to encourage real participation. Although we used Pascal and Bertram's descriptors in the pilot phase of our research, it seemed to us that this was a critical area for development in our own study. We were not simply concerned with defining appropriate adult engagement styles in terms of the role of the early childhood educator. We were also concerned with the adult engagement styles in terms of how parents, as the child's first educator, could most effectively engage with their children in the home setting.

Developing our own categories of effective teaching strategies

Instead of focusing, as so often seems to happen, on what parents were not doing well, we decided it would be salutary to build on what parents were doing really well. The parents involved in the project agreed that nursery staff could video them interacting with their children in the nursery early in the morning during the settling in period. Subsequently nursery staff were also videoed working with the same children.

Obstacles to progress

We were aware that during the first phase of the project nursery staff were often reluctant to be filmed. In fact, we had many hours of videotape in which the nursery resembled the Marie Celeste with all the adults having abandoned ship! It was clear that staff consistently avoided being in front of the camera.

At this point we came across the work of Maggie Haggerty (1996) in New Zealand who had produced, for her MA dissertation, evidence relating to the same problem. (Maggie Haggerty had worked with student teachers in New Zealand who experienced many of the same anxieties expressed by our staff group). At Pen Green we decided to run a training day with an external consultant to discuss and debate all the issues nursery staff had about being filmed, and about filming other people. Working together with the parents, staff acknowledged their fears and anxieties, which included:

- their feelings about being judged by others;
- their issues about power, particularly the power of the person holding the camera;
- their issues about personal shyness; and
- their issues about how their performance was affected by the pressure of being videoed.

A plan was drawn up for the rest of the research programme and all the nursery staff agreed that they would be filmed working with at least one of the research project children over an eight-week period. They decided to set up a 'buddy' system so that they filmed and were filmed by a colleague in whom they had a high degree of confidence. Each member of the nursery staff was filmed with a project child and then they (or a colleague) filmed the child with his or her parent at the beginning of each nursery session. At the end of this period we had made 16 video vignettes of nursery staff and parents working with individual project children. Staff then agreed to continue to use the 'buddy' system we had developed so that they could make videos of all the other project children during the spring term.

The parents did not, in the main, express the same kind of

reservations as the nursery staff about being videoed. Since all new parents settle their children into nursery for a two-week period they were accustomed to the nursery routine at the beginning of the day. Most parents regularly spend time at the beginning of each day settling the children in and because of the flexible start (parents can bring children in from 8.15 a.m. onwards) this was a relatively relaxed and unpressured time in nursery. It seemed that the reservations and anxieties parents would naturally feel on interacting with their children had been regularly worked through on these occasions and they had a high degree of confidence in the staff. They did not feel that staff were making negative judgements about their parenting styles. Accordingly, the pressure of the camera's presence did not seem to have the same impact on parents.

Video analysis session

On the last day of the autumn term we held an informal video analysis session for both nursery staff and project parents. On this occasion, we wanted the nursery staff and parents to view the video clips as empirical data that needed to be closely observed and then analysed. We decided to try out a new approach (Jordan and Henderson, 1995) to watching and analysing the tapes. Staff and parents shared a meal together, and then sat down in front of the video screen. We set aside a two and a half hour session with one and a half hours of video clips to view. The agreement between staff and parents was that we would watch the clips and anyone could ask for the tape to be stopped if:

- they wanted to discuss what they had observed; or
- wanted clarification about what individual staff or parents were doing on the tape.

The only caveat was that the ensuing discussion could only be sustained for five minutes, after which we had to once again focus on the video-taped evidence. We could either go back over a controversial clip or move on to look at a new clip. In this way, we could make sure that the dialogical process (Freire, 1970) was grounded in the evidence base of the tapes, rather than on preconceived assumptions.

The video analysis group comprised the children's parents and their key workers. We watched the videos in sequence so that we saw a particular child interacting first with her parents and then with her key worker. Staff were intrigued by the fact that they sometimes appeared to unconsciously mimic parental patterns of behaviour when they were trying to engage particular children within their key worker group. Some staff expressed anxieties about this and were concerned that parents might feel they were usurping the parental role; parents, however, reassured them and affirmed how much they valued staff developing warm, responsive relationships with their children. Parents began to comment on their own styles of interacting with their children and were keen to explain why they had behaved in certain ways at certain times.

We hoped that through this discussion we would be able to identify consistent behaviour, and differences in behaviour. We hoped to identify strengths in both parents' and staff's interventions. We wanted to consider how we could build on best practice to enhance the children's learning at home and in nursery.

Inevitably, even though we had allowed two and a half hours, we were only able to review approximately 20 minutes of the tape in the first session! The level of debate and discussion was very high. Over the next two to three weeks we completed three extended video analysis sessions. At the end of these discussions, we were able to identify some key features in the behaviour parents exhibited when interacting with their children in nursery:

- anticipation – parents seemed intuitively to know what to do next when a child needed something physically or emotionally;
- recall – the parents could share past experiences and relate them to what the children were doing or saying now while they played;
- mirroring experience through language – parents would verbally reflect back to the children what they were doing;
- extending experiences and accompanying the child – parents were quick to think about and show children new ways to approach things. They were also willing to allow their children's interest and give them the time and space to explore things;
- asking the child's view – parents seemed interested in what their children were thinking and feeling about things;
- encouraging autonomy – parents encouraged their children to make choices and decisions;
- boundary-setting/encouraging risk-taking – parents seem to know when to step in and how to encourage their children to have a go; and
- judicious use of experience of failure/making mistakes – parents supported their children's right to experiment, to make mistakes and occasionally experience failure.

Developing the pedagogic strategies

A small group of nursery staff working with our pedagogic consultant, Professor Tina Bruce, spent many hours trying to identify underlying processes and the overt and conscious teaching strategies that both parents and nursery staff had used. Our aim was to develop a framework for effective teaching strategies. We wanted to develop categories that would help us to identify different pedagogical approaches and assess their effectiveness.

The categories needed to illustrate the complexity of the adult interventions. At the same time the framework for observation needed to be a relatively simple tool, one that could be used regularly in our observations of each other, and of the parents. After a great deal of struggle with different forms of conceptual mapping we did establish a set of fairly simple descriptors which illustrated complex interactions. The eight pedagogic strategies that follow are drawn from our observations of the different kinds of behaviour demonstrated by parents and nursery staff:

Effective pedagogic strategies

1   Subtle intervention
2   Knowledge of the child's embedded context, and ability to recall the child's previous experience
3   Affirmation of the child through facial expression and physical closeness
4   Encouraging children to make choices and decisions
5   The adult supports the child to take appropriate risks
6   The adult encourages the child to go beyond the adult's own knowledge base and accompany them into new experiences
7   The adult has an awareness of the impact of their own attitudes and beliefs and how these might affect the child's learning
8   The adult demonstrates learning as a partnership; the adult is committed to their own learning and generates a spirit of enquiry

(Whalley and Arnold, 1997b).

Subtle intervention

Staff and parents were all very aware of the danger of a 'hands on' approach where the adult's 'hands on' inhibits the children's learning. We had all watched video clips where inappropriate actions on the part of adults clearly took the initiative away from the child. Sometimes the child's physical space was imposed on and they were hurried along from activity to activity within an adult determined timescale.

There were some subtle differences in the way that parents and staff intervened. Some parents seemed, at times, to be able to anticipate the next step that would keep their child engaged that little bit longer. Other parents knew just when to gently divert the child's attention so that their emotional needs were met and at the same time they could continue to learn.

For the nursery staff, subtle intervention was often about waiting and watching before intervening. It involved the adult maintaining a respectful distance until the child was clearly signalling that they needed help. It was about supporting and encouraging the child to the point at which they were excited by the struggle and the intensity of the challenge, then moving in gently to extend the learning.

Staff at staff meetings extended their understanding of subtle intervention through discussions of Bruner's concept of 'scaffolding learning' (Bruner, 1977), Vygotsky's zone of proximal development (Vygotsky, 1978) and Bruce's concept of 'match plus one' (Bruce, 1997).

We shared the view with parents that an overzealous focus on teaching could inhibit the children's learning. What worked best for children was an approach that combined observation, subtle intervention and reflection.

Knowledge of the child's embedded context and the ability to recall the child's previous experience

From our observations of parents and nursery workers, it seemed that parents had a decided advantage in terms of their in-depth knowledge of their child's recent and relevant experiences. Often 2- and 3-year-olds would try hard to communicate important contextual information to staff about things they had done last night or at 'nanna's' and they were not always able to make themselves understood. Parents, however, were able to recognize what the children wanted to say and help them to articulate their experience, gently prompting them, at times, to assist them when they were trying to recall experiences over an extended period of time.

Since Pen Green nursery staff regularly home visit the children in their key worker groups, they do have some understanding of the child's home environment, and will probably know many of the important adults in the child's life. However, this was something that staff had to work at, whereas for parents it came quite naturally. Staff sometimes needed to make life books, with photographs of family members or home to nursery link books, to keep in touch with the important people and events in the children's life. Once again this kind of information was not as subtle, nor as intimate, as the knowledge held by parents, knowledge that could be built on to support and extend the children's learning. For example, Chelsea had gone to visit relatives in Scotland and had taken a much-loved bag full of her favourite toys and her make-up box. She saw it disappear down the conveyor belt, which carried the baggage out to the plane, and had been wild with excitement when she came back to nursery to share the experience. With support from her father, Warren, she was able to share the formative experience of seeing her baggage disappear, reclaiming it and share her fascination about the conveyor belt that had carried it away. Staff and her parents were able to build on this information and extend her learning by visiting a much more complex conveyor belt in the Science Museum.

Affirmation of the child through facial expression and physical closeness

There were striking differences in the way that key workers and parents physically related to the children. Kristen, Naomi's mother, settled Naomi into nursery by encouraging her to play with the blocks, a favourite occupation. Naomi became absorbed quite quickly and Kristen sat very close by but to one side of Naomi. Kristen gave Naomi all her attention and quietly played alongside until it was time for her to leave. A taped sequence of Naomi with her family worker (key worker) showed a very different scenario. Karen, Naomi's key worker, sits, physically, very close to Naomi while she is playing in a sandpit; other children move in and out and Naomi repeatedly goes up to Karen to make sure that she has her full attention. At one point Naomi physically touches Karen's face to redirect her gaze. It seemed that in many of the video clips family workers had to work physically closer to the children to reassure them and affirm that contact between adult and child. The children seemed to be fairly confident that their parents were there for them and at times were rather less confident that they had the undivided attention of the nursery worker. Perhaps reasonably so, in that, at least for the duration of the settling in period, the parents were very much focusing on one child whereas nursery workers had to constantly respond to a minimum of four other children, and often many more. Parents often demonstrated a physical closeness to the children but, to be effective, staff almost always had to engage closely with the children if the play was to develop and to be sustained.

Encouraging the children to make choices and decisions

Staff and parents avoided overdirecting the children. At the start of the day the children were gently introduced to different areas within the nursery by their parents; both staff and parents were willing to follow the children's lead and accommodate their interests. It was obvious that for some children a side-by-side approach with the key worker gradually taking over the support role as the child's parents withdrew was the best way to accomplish a smooth transition into nursery. With other children it was important to immediately establish peer support and assist them in finding their best friend before they could accept their parent's departure.

Some children came to nursery knowing exactly how they wanted to spend their time and the adults would encourage them in that decision-making process. For example, Harry sometimes hid a favourite piece of Brio underneath a cupboard; whilst accepting that he could not take toys out of nursery he was determined not to be thwarted in his extended play with the track and trains. Alice *needed* to sit on the rocking horse where she could watch her mother leave. From this secure vantage point she could, with the support of her family worker, identify in which workshop area of the nursery she wanted to start her day. Zaki, knowing that the minibus would go out most days, would take responsibility for the clipboard and identify whose turn it was to go out and negotiate the destination.

Encouraging decision-making is a key feature of the nursery philosophy and it became obvious from this shared piece of work that parents were, on the whole, prepared to give the children time to learn how to make good choices.

The adult supports the child in taking appropriate risks

In our analysis of the parents' interactions that we had on video, we noticed a huge strength in the parents' ability to encourage and support the children in experimentation. The parents were able to support their children's right to experiment, make mistakes and occasionally experience failure, and we needed to be equally aware, in the nursery, of the value of a 'judicious' measure of risk-taking and making mistakes. Parents seemed accustomed to diverting children when the experience of failure was overwhelming and were very committed to allowing children several 'shots' at a task before they gave up. Sometimes nursery staff were overanxious and overprotective perhaps because their ability to comfort the child, if things went wrong, was not as great as that of most of the parents. On some occasions, however, the parents were more anxious than the nursery staff, for example over the use of scissors in the nursery or when children were pouring drinks. Children who are overwatched and assessed to be incompetent will inevitably spill their juice and drop the tray of cups they are carrying even when they do, in fact, have the competence to carry out these tasks.

Risk-taking at a deep level, such as permitting nursery age children to stay away overnight at a well-organized farm holiday, was something that daunted both parents and staff but the 3- and 4-year-olds who participated gained enormously despite all our shared anxieties.

The adult encourages the child to go beyond the adult's own knowledge base and accompany them into new experiences

At times both staff and parents struggled to understand the children's persistent concerns. On many video clips the adults watched the children deeply engaged in activities that were hard to define. For instance, when children were intent on sellotaping around the door handles and then connecting doors up and down the corridor with Sellotape and, subsequently, with string. However, parents and staff were able to watch respectfully and follow-up the observations with dialogue and adult level investigation. Staff and parents both drew on their knowledge about the Leuven Involvement Levels and watching children who were clearly deeply involved were prepared to suspend 'disbelief' and encourage the children to develop their cognitive concerns even when what they were doing was, at times, challenging. Children with beetle brows and tongues sticking out between their teeth, intent on making some new discovery, were generally supported in their task. The adults supporting them often had to dialogue at length, study key texts and go with hunches to accompany the children into new experiences.

On one memorable occasion, Alice became deeply involved in conveyor belts (see Chapter 8 for Alice's portfolio). She had been taken to see a conveyor belt at the Science Museum and was keen to understand how it worked. Staff improvised a conveyor belt in the nursery through securing paper around a table top and she spent hours intently learning how to manoeuvre the belt and watching objects move along it and drop into the metal container. Having experimented with many solid objects she finally experimented with a spherical ball and she (and the nursery staff) stood by perplexed when, unlike all the solid objects, the ball failed to drop off the conveyor belt. At three years six months Alice had a 'false hypothesis' (Harlen, 1982) that all objects would follow the same laws and move forward and drop off the end of the conveyor belt and most of the staff shared her view! Other staff had a very vague awareness of forces, gravity and the laws of motion which were, indeed, in operation and much discussion was needed before we could successfully extend Alice's learning opportunities appropriately.

The adult has an awareness of the impact of their own attitudes and beliefs and how these might affect the child's learning

Staff and parents had to work hard to develop their understanding about how their own values and beliefs and attitudes were impacting on, and sometimes inhibiting, the child's right to learn. We all became aware that overanxiety was a common feature of staff's and parents' behaviour. The overwatched child who was always offered assistance when climbing the trees in the nursery garden or when experimenting on the climbing frame could not develop a sense of competence and confidence as a climber. Girls dressed in skirts and dresses were almost always at a disadvantage and were more often than not offered assistance by our largely female staff group. In Loris Malaguzzi's words, 'every child has the right to be away from the ever watchful eye of the adult' (Malaguzzi, 1992, personal discussion).

Sometimes our debates and struggle over values and beliefs went even deeper. One parent experiencing an overwhelmingly painful separation from a partner had chosen to tell her nursery child that his Daddy was 'dead'. In fact, his father was well known in the community and passed the nursery every day and had no contact with the child. Another parent, who was pregnant herself, was not permitted, within her own religion and culture, to share with her son information about how the baby was progressing which nursery staff would have considered to be appropriate. Paradoxically her son's nursery worker was pregnant at the same time and all the other children in his key worker group would pat their nursery worker's tummy and eagerly ask questions about what was going on. Faced with these value-based dilemmas, staff and parents shared their views and feelings respectfully. Whilst, in many cases, there was no easy reconciliation of different view points, the issue of children's rights was at least aired, and the best possible practice was ensured.

The adult demonstrates learning as a partnership; the adult is committed to their own learning and generates a spirit of enquiry

Despite the fact that many of the parents were juggling with bringing up a family, part-time or full-time work and coping on a low income, it was clear that, without exception, they had aspirations for their children and were anxious to support them in any way that they could. They responded to the challenge of videoing their children and thinking about their learning with as much enthusiasm as the nursery staff. Many of them were stimulated by their involvement in the project, and in the nursery generally, to go back to study or to pick up a half-completed course.

Staff became aware of huge gaps in their own learning particularly in the area of science and mathematics, and much of our in-service training over the last three years has focused on these areas of the curriculum. In Chapter 2 we described how nursery staff had been deeply concerned about a disengaged group of 4-year-old boys who always seemed to be 'roaming in gangs' around the nursery around February or March each year. It cannot be coincidental that when staff became highly tuned into the children's need to develop their understanding of scientific and mathematical concepts and increased their own skills and competences in these areas then these kinds of negative behaviours diminished. Most staff undertook further or higher education courses and training was given a high priority at Pen Green. Wherever possible staff who undertook training in their own time were financially supported, given some time back and offered 'time out' to complete assignments.

Involving fathers and male carers

At Pen Green we have worked hard for a number of years to tackle issues of gender stereotyping (Ghedini *et al.*, 1995, p. 36). In a review of our work with fathers in 1990 we found that local fathers often failed to get involved in services and were either excluded by other parents or excluded themselves. For example, when the staff at the Centre decided to positively encourage fathers to settle their children in nursery and worked hard to engage the fathers during the two week settling in period, 87 per cent of fathers turned up. In our discussions with parents mothers initially assumed that their partners did not want to be involved, and the fathers assumed that their partners did not want them to be involved. In the vast majority of cases these assumptions were not well founded.

Pen Green Centre's work to include fathers has met with some success. Fathers particularly enjoy attending meetings which focused on science and technology. One father spent 40 minutes exploring our key concepts CD-ROM at a parents' evening and said, the next day, that the information he had acquired had revolutionized the way that he saw his son's play.

The establishment of the research base in the Centre has led to a further increase in the involvement of fathers. It was clear from the beginning that if the research to study parents' involvement in their children's learning was to be successful then it was vital to involve fathers and other primary male carers in the work.

Extending the research to explore fathers'/male carers' engagement styles

Although there were two fathers involved in the original pilot project and a significant number of fathers involved in the second year, the video observations that informed our framework for pedagogic strategies only included one father. We had not, at that time, considered the particular qualities that fathers might bring to their role. It seemed to us important to replicate our work with a group of fathers.

Using the framework we had already developed on effective pedagogical strategies we looked at the interactions between fathers and children in the nursery. The fathers who were invited to be part of this project had already demonstrated an interest in knowing more about their children's play in nursery and were happy to let us video them settling their children into nursery.

Six fathers got involved. It was interesting to note that all these fathers had been present at their children's birth and felt that this experience had had a strong emotional impact on their lives. Two of the fathers had two sons and found interesting parallels between their children. Both had older sons who they described as typical boys, that is loud, noisy and needed to run about a lot and play rough and tumble games. Their younger sons were quieter, enjoyed drawing and stories. Those fathers that had more than one child often struggled with sharing their time between their two children.

The fathers who became involved (Figure 5.1) were:

- Alex, who is married with one daughter, Chloe. Alex and his partner are both in full-time employment;
- Rory, who is married with a daughter, Lindsey. Rory and his partner both work;
- Lewis, who is separated, has two sons, is unemployed and shares the care of the children;
- Dave, who is married with one son and one daughter, is in full-time employment and his partner also works away from the home;
- Marcus, who has three children, lives with his partner and is employed in the nursery full time; and
- Nick, who is married with two children and both parents are employed.

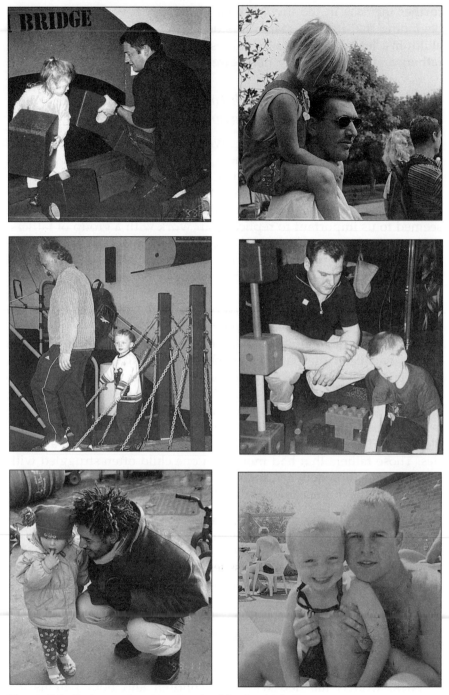

Figure 5.1 Fathers who were involved in the project

Three of the fathers, Alex, Rory and Lewis, were recorded as they settled their children into the nursery before going to work. Alex stayed
with his daughter, Chloe, for 30 minutes whilst she was deeply
engaged in block play; Rory chatted to his daughter, Lindsey, and
Lewis helped his son, Aaron, on the nursery computer and encouraged another boy to join him. Dave was video-filmed as he sat with
two children and read them a story whilst sitting on a sofa. Dave
already works in the nursery on a sessional basis to gain experience
of working in an early years setting as he is planning to make a career
change and study for an NVQ in Education and Childcare. His own
child also attends the nursery. Marcus, a family worker in the nursery, sat with two nursery children playing with dough, cooking uten-
sils and cones. Marcus is a full-time member of the nursery staff and
his own child attended the nursery. Nick was filmed as he helped the
children empty and clean out the fish tank.

Analysing the videotapes

Two of the Centre staff met with four out of the six fathers to analyse
the video recordings that we made (two of the fathers were unable to
meet because of work commitments). The purpose of the meeting
with the fathers was to look at the nature of their interactions with
their children. We also wanted to see if our framework of pedagogic
strategies was as relevant to men working with children as it was for
women working with children. In other words, were the pedagogic
strategies gender neutral or were there were gender specific differences?

David (1994) reflects on this issue when she notes that research on
mothers and fathers concentrates too much on what fathers do in
comparison with mothers, rather than on the quality of their time with
children. 'What may be more important is their sensitivity (or not) to
their child during such interactions' (David, 1994, p. 6).

From our shared analysis session, we made the following observations and identified some key issues.

Subtle intervention – fathers interacting with children gently and respectfully

All six fathers demonstrated this quality and it was particularly strong
in four of the six observations that were made. The first two examples illustrate what is meant by subtle intervention when fathers are
interacting with their children or indeed with other children in the
nursery.

Example 1 Dave, who was sitting on the sofa in the nursery, is reading a story to Jessica. She is sitting on his lap in a very relaxed way. They are both involved in the story when Christopher walks up to them and sits beside Dave on the sofa. Dave invites Christopher to join them in the story and notices that Christopher has a plastic apron on, which is uncomfortable now that he is sitting down. He offers to help Christopher take off the apron and with his agreement does so. Christopher now chooses to sit by Dave and involves himself in the story. During this important interaction with Christopher, Dave maintains eye contact with Jessica and talks to her. He shows awareness of both children's needs and is able to engage and maintain their interest in the story.

Example 2 Alex is with his daughter in the block-play area. Chloe is very involved in building with the blocks. Alex maintains a discreet distance from her when she is using the blocks in a competent way. He is very quick to intervene when she gets stuck and she asks for help. Her request for help is both verbal and through eye contact. They are very much in tune with each other's signals. She asks for help when she could not get a block out of the shelf because they were too tightly packed and Alex intervenes when he sees that the task is too difficult for her. When she tries to stand on a round block and she finds it difficult to keep her balance, Alex very quickly moves in to hold her hand and allow her to experiment safely.

Fathers demonstrate knowledge of their children's previous experiences and interests and/or current concerns

This strategy was demonstrated in all the observations, whether it was with the father's own children or other children in the nursery.

Example 3 When we are looking at the video together, Alex picks out the way that his daughter Chloe is walking with a long block in the block area. She is banging it up and down and walking with a stoop. He remarks that both Chloe's grandmothers use walking sticks and she seems to be incorporating this into her block play.

Example 4 Rory fixes the button on Lindsey's dungarees. In doing so he celebrates with Lindsey the fact that she dresses herself in the morning and does it very well. He plays a counting game with her by asking her how many names she, her mum and her dad have. She then goes through everyone's names.

Fathers show that they appreciate the child's efforts and wants to support them by getting physically close, working physically alongside and through positive reassuring facial expressions

Fathers in many of the video sequences clearly enjoyed being physically close to their children and were physically responsive and sensitive to their children's need for truth and reassurance.

Example 5 Nick moved in and out of being physically close. This may have been due to the activity that he was involved in, which was emptying the fish tank. It is interesting to note that when Nick was standing at the sink and involved in a conversation with another adult for a brief time the children's level of involvement dropped quite noticeably. Nick was, however, quick to pick this up and squatted down to talk to the children. The children's level of involvement in the activity increased when he was actively engaging them.

Example 6 Rory remained physically distant from his daughter. He remained standing throughout their time together, often with his arms folded. He was, however, able to engage his daughter in conversation even at a distance and sustained good eye contact with her with a lot of smiles and laughter exchanged between them. As he was about to leave Lindsey he touched her face and they kissed goodbye.

Example 7 Lewis is with his son, Aaron, and another boy, Samuel, on the computer. Both Lewis and Aaron are sitting in chairs of their own whilst Samuel stands beside Lewis. They are all three very focused on the computer screen and Lewis is sharing the mouse with the children. There is little eye contact between them while they are focused on the computer. However, there is one point where Lewis takes over the mouse from Aaron to achieve a task that they are sharing. Aaron appears to lose interest in the activity at this point and he makes a move to walk down to nursery. Lewis disengages himself from the computer and gently touches Aaron on the arm to gain his attention. Aaron then returns to the computer task at Lewis's invitation.

Lewis also invites Samuel to sit on his knee so that he can reach the mouse and see the computer screen more easily.

Fathers respect their children's right to make choices and decisions
The video recordings showed many instances of the fathers showing sensitivity to the children in terms of when to intervene and when to leave the children to carry on independently.

The fathers discussed this particular strategy at length. All the fathers believed in respecting children's rights to make their own choices and decisions. They did, however, say that this was hard to achieve. For example, when they had to go to work, they would do tasks for their children in order to get them to nursery on time. They felt that the times when they were with their children without having to be anywhere at a particular moment were very precious.

Example 8 Nick moves in and out of supporting the children to siphon the water off. He explains the importance of keeping the tube submerged in the water. The children experiment with taking the tube out to see what happens. The children are experimenting through direct experience and are in control of what they are doing in this complex task.

Example 9 Marcus always checks with the children when he intervenes to help them and never takes any intervention for granted. He offers the children different materials to use in their play which they accept or reject. They usually accept what he offers and his interventions are always in keeping with what the children are doing. His interventions extend the children's play and do not disrupt the flow of their play.

Example 10 When reading the story to Christopher and Jessica, Dave responds to their questions and requests. When Christopher first joins in the story he wants to turn the pages very quickly before hearing the story in detail. Dave allows him to do this rather than telling him to wait and listen to the story. Dave remains child focused rather than task focused.

Fathers encourage and support their children to take risks appropriately
There were very few obvious examples of risk-taking in the video observations. In our discussions as a staff group and with the fathers we discussed the concept of 'risk-taking'. What may seem like an ordinary, safe, day-to-day activity to the casual observer, can for an individual be a huge personal risk. For Christopher, aged 3, to interrupt the storytelling between Dave and Jessica may have been a big risk.

Chloe took risks in building a tower with the blocks until they collapsed. She looked over to her Dad when this happened and was reassured by his response that it was okay.

Some fathers felt that they were at times overprotective towards their children. It was not always easy in practice to know when intervention was helpful and when it was either controlling or disempowering for the child. Fathers said that they felt as protective towards their sons as their daughters and they were also aware of their children's different emotional needs.

Fathers encourage the children to get involved in deep-level learning that goes beyond what the adult already knows; fathers support/accompany them in their play/learning

This strategy was the one that gave rise to most discussion. Most of the fathers said they had not experienced their children raising any questions that they did not know the answers to! They had a range of strategies for explaining things to their children. One father said that he would make up stories to answer his children's questions. These stories were used to explain what the child wanted to know in terms that the father thought he would understand. Another father said that he responded by giving the facts in as straightforward a way as possible; if he felt that the explanation would be problematic then he would change the subject.

Those fathers in the group who attended the key concept training days on the curriculum had found them very useful as they felt that they understood more clearly how their children were involved in learning through their play.

> *Example 11* Christopher is pretending to make cakes with the dough. Marcus, his nursery worker, joins in with the play through pretending to eat the cake when Christopher gives him a bit. He extends Christopher's learning by introducing a rolling pin and showing him how to flatten the dough. Christopher is deeply involved in the play which reflects his interest and level of learning. Marcus also shows Christopher that one side of the pastry cutter is sharper than the other and that it is easier to cut the dough with the sharp edge. Christopher continues to use the pastry cutter in a more appropriate way with considerable satisfaction.

Fathers appear to be aware that what they say and how they behave reflects their own attitudes and beliefs, and this has an effect on what the child is able to learn from them and share with them

Through their interactions with the children all the fathers showed a high degree of sensitivity. This was reflected in the degree of non-verbal communication that was put into practice, for example, getting down physically to the child's level, good eye contact and using a tone of voice that was soft and animated. The language they used was clearly pitched at a level the children could understand and was concerned with the children's interests. Alex, in Example 1, was very concerned that his daughter had the right to take the lead in her play, although, in fact, what Chloe, his daughter, wanted was an equal and active partnership. Sometimes she took the lead, sometimes she watched her Dad and sometimes they both played together.

Example 12 Alex decided to allow himself to be observed through the video recording because he understood that his daughter, Chloe, was deeply involved in block play when he brought her into nursery. Throughout her play he maintains a distance and is respectful of his daughter's personal space so that she can develop her play.

Chloe is confident and playful in her block play. She pushes her building to the limit and celebrates her achievements with her Dad and members of staff. She is not discouraged when her building collapses. She works and plays with confidence knowing that her Dad is there to support her and she has his complete attention. When he tells her that he has to leave and go to work, she protests and then accepts that he needs to go. After he has gone Chloe returns to her block play and continues to build.

Fathers work alongside the child as a resourceful friend and partner in their learning; the adult enjoys learning in his own right and is curious and wants to know more

The fathers involved in this research were very much in agreement with the idea of the adult as a resourceful friend, however, they struggled with the idea that they needed to develop their own learning. They wanted to develop their understanding of how children learn and wanted to know how they could help their children learn. They did not feel that their children challenged in any way their understanding of the world around them.

Fathers communicating with their children

An analysis of the fathers' use of language showed that the amount of language used varied considerably. Two fathers talked with their children much of the time in their interactions with one of them using very little physical contact. Another father used very little language but was physically very close to the children and involved in the activity alongside them. All the fathers used language to explain things and extend children's learning. One father was very good at using language to reflect back to the child what the child was doing. Two of the fathers were fairly task centred in the activity they were involved in and used language to encourage the children to complete the task.

There was also a lot of eye contact between all the fathers and the children they were working with. The children showed themselves to be very comfortable with physical contact with the fathers. The fathers responded sensitively to the children who set their own boundaries in terms of proximity and touch.

Issues that arose

The range of adult pedagogic strategies the fathers used were very similar to those we had noted in mothers at an earlier stage in the project. Differences often seemed to be more closely linked to personality than to gender. However there *was* a difference in the fathers' perceptions of how far their own knowledge and understanding might be challenged by the child. It seemed that these fathers accepted their roles and responsibilities as teachers or first educators but did not see themselves as 'learners'.

The process of involving fathers in their children's learning is one that has to be constantly reviewed and negotiated. The fathers' response to this and other work has been very positive and demonstrates that fathers as well as mothers care passionately about their children's emotional and cognitive needs. The work at Pen Green Centre and, in particular, the research base has shown that parents, regardless of gender, class, ethnicity, have a genuine desire to be involved in their children's development and want to work in a genuine partnership with early years professionals.

There are enormous benefits to identifying a close working partnership between parents and early years workers:

- Parents benefit from increasing their knowledge and understanding of their children through group discussion with other parents and staff.
- Staff benefit through increasing their knowledge and understanding of the children's learning opportunities at home; their ability to provide continuity and new experiences for the child within the nursery is then extended.
- Children benefit because the significant adults in their lives are able to provide richer learning opportunities.
- Children also experience their parents and carers working closely together. This gives them a sense of continuity and of being cared for, and creates a trusting and secure environment in which they can learn and grow.

6

Persistence Pays Off: Working with 'Hard to Reach' Parents

Cath Arnold

This chapter looks at what these particular parents have in common with each other, why we want to engage all parents of nursery children and how we adapt our methods to ensure that we are giving all the parents equal opportunities to be involved in their children's learning. The chapter draws on two parents' stories of their own educational experience as children and adults.

The background

As part of the Parents' Involvement in their Children's Learning project, we carry out a semi-structured interview with each of our nursery parents each year. We are aware that Corby has among its total population very few adults who go on to further or higher education (Corby Sure Start Bid, internal document produced for the DfEE Sure Start Unit in 1999). We feel that this is likely to have a significant affect on the parents' aspirations for their children. Therefore we ask the parents about their own experiences of education during the interview. Often parents will expand on this by telling us more about their educational experiences during the interview or informally afterwards. A substantial number of parents interviewed (approx 30 per cent) have expressed their dissatisfaction particularly with the secondary phase of their schooling. A small number (6 per cent) were frequently excluded or suspended from school or were habitual truants. Either way, this small group of parents missed a substantial amount of schooling and, consequently, have had very little experience of achievement as children.

In the past, the anti-social acts which lead to exclusions have sometimes been viewed as the fault of the children or their families. The educational underachievement of children from working-class families was seen by sociologists in the 1960s as 'their inability to defer gratification' or as 'a lower priority placed upon educational success' (Abbott, 1998, p. 65). Abbott, however, argues that, 'It might be the case that working class parents were unconfident in their ability to deal adequately with the norms and values of schools and teachers' (ibid.). There was a feeling that schools and teachers knew best and only by conforming to their rules and values would pupils succeed.

What was not always acknowledged was that the expectations that teachers and schools have of their pupils and their families affect how those pupils feel and act (Faulkner, 1995). Whalley (1992, p. 199) observed in a case study of a day nursery and nursery unit that, 'Day nursery staff and nursery unit staff viewed their parents as somewhere on a range with abusive and neglectful at one extreme and poor and disadvantaged at the other. It becomes clear why the amount of parental involvement in this and other studies correlates with staff attitudes towards parents'. The judgements made by staff of parents affect how the family feels about school and, possibly, create a barrier to becoming more involved with school or education in general.

Why we want to engage all parents

Having an Equal Opportunities Policy does not necessarily mean that we offer equal opportunities to all families. We realize that we are working towards offering each child and family an equal opportunity to education and care. Parents are all different and, therefore, to make the provision accessible to all families means that we are constantly questioning our ways of engaging parents (Whalley, 1997b). Each child is entitled to have his or her parents involved in his or her education and we have a duty to provide the means by which parents are able to be involved. We have found that offering different ways to become involved, at different times of day and with a crèche, helps (see Chapter 4).

Longitudinal research studies give strong evidence that involving parents in their children's education benefits the children, their families and society (Athey, 1990; Rutter and Rutter, 1992; Easen, Kendall and Shaw,1992; Fuerst and Fuerst, 1993; Weinberger, 1996). From a purely financial viewpoint, it is claimed that for every $1 spent on early education, $7 are saved because students are well adjusted citizens and have a better quality of life (Sylva, 1999). A similar claim is being made (*TES* 2000, p. 11) about Early Excellence Centres in the UK: 'Preliminary research by University College Worcester shows for every £1 invested in early excellence centres, £8 is saved on alternative services such as foster care and counselling.'

Sylva is concerned with assessing the 'quality' of early education on offer to the child. The Early Excellence evaluation programme is concerned with the quality of services to the whole family. Projects which involve parents and local communities in decision-making seem to have the most long-term impact on children and their families. Community projects from as far afield as Venezuela, India and South Africa confirm that involving parents and the local community is the key to helping children to achieve their potential both educationally and socially (Atmore, 1999; Sood, 1999; Yanez, 1999).

Athey (1990, p. 20) makes the point that, 'Most research in the 1960's and 70's was designed to assist the inadequate parent'. Parents were taught 'parenting skills' by experts. It was believed that child-rearing skills could be transmitted to parents by telling them what to do and encouraging them to practise. The rich experience of bringing up their own children from birth, which parents brought to the learning situation, was not acknowledged as important. In the Froebel Early Education Project (Athey, 1990) the agenda was still set by the educators. However, the parents' contribution to professional knowledge about each child was acknowledged. During the 1980s and 1990s there has been some shift in thinking in the sense that parents are recognized at least in government rhetoric as 'experts on their own children' (Athey, 1990, p. 61). Many parenting programmes still work from the premise that there are a lot of parenting skills that should be taught to 'less effective' parents.

Shaw (1991), working in the tradition of Athey and Bruce, set up a home-visiting project in the North East of England. The six families that Shaw worked with were described as 'vulnerable'. They all lived in the 'inner city' and were 'unemployed and had limited resources available to them, materially and in terms of their own previous education' (Shaw, 1991, p. 105). In addition, all of the families were living in 'highly stressful circumstances' (ibid.). Despite their individual needs, 'The agenda for discussion was negotiated between the parents and researcher' (Easen, Kendall and Shaw, 1992, pp. 282–96).

Shaw offered the parents a schematic interpretation of their children's actions, which enabled the parents to have an alternative way of understanding their children's actions. This led to the parents reflecting on their own education and upbringing. Shaw discovered that,

'Unremarkably, the parents' learning process appears to be similar to the child's learning process as described by Athey; that is, both children and parents have developed cognitive structures which have built up from experience and which underpin behaviour. First hand experience is therefore central to the learning process for children and parents'.

(Easen, Kendall and Shaw, 1992, p. 287)

Watching their own children and discussing what might be happening with the researcher, resulted in the parents and the researcher gaining knowledge and seeing things 'in new ways' (Easen, Kendall and Shaw, 1992, p. 288). Mezirow (1977) calls this process 'perspective transformation'. Because perspectives have 'dimensions of thought, feelings and will' people begin to see things differently and to behave differently (Mezirow, 1977, p. 158).

In a similar way, our evidence shows that parents, who have become involved in the Parents' Involvement in their Children's Learning project, are seeing their children's development and learning in a new 'light'. Our aim is to give all our nursery parents opportunities to become involved in the ways that suit them best.

Early in the project it became apparent that *all* of our parents are potential participants. The respect we show for the parents' prior knowledge and experience can make a difference to how they feel about themselves and about their children. Easen *et al.* (1992, p. 294) comment, 'Through the validation of their experience, parents' self-esteem and confidence in their role as a parent and as an individual is enhanced'. Whalley (1997b, p. 92) makes a similar point, 'Parents need to know that staff care about them as well as their children'.

We were aware of parents using the Centre facilities, who had had poor experiences of education and schooling during their own childhoods and we very much wanted to improve opportunities for them and their children.

This small group of parents attending Pen Green Centre, who were excluded from school or were habitual truants, can give us an insight into what happened from their perspective. Two mothers, who are regular users of the Centre, agreed to tell the stories of their own education and they also agreed to share their views about what they want from the education system for their children. Both parents checked the full transcript of their own story.

These two parents have been involved in the PICL project, but only in a peripheral way. One of the parents attended a study group for six months and came to various other meetings and events. The other parent became involved on a one-to-one basis but did not sustain involvement with the group over time.

Jack (1987, p. 102) says, 'The oral interview not only allows women to articulate their own experiences but also to reflect upon the meaning of those experiences to them'. Rather than make speculations, as educators, about the reasons for exclusions and truanting, we wanted to be able to listen to their actual experiences and to 'construct our theories out of the actual experiences' (Wittner, 1987, p. 105).

These two stories are individual representations of the experiences of two parents and may help us to gain further insights about how we, as educators, can adapt our organizations and behaviour to accommodate the needs of a wider range of children and parents. Tracey and Kate represent a minority group. Laevers (1995) refers to 'children who fall out of the boat' and this description seems to fit their childhood experiences.

What is different or special about these parents

The two parents interviewed are parents who have been regular users of some of the Centre's facilities for some years. One has attended the youth club in the Centre and then had a child in the nursery for two years. The other parent has frequently used the family room (a room where parents can drop in and chat to other parents) over a number of years, and has had two children attend the nursery. We feel that we know both of these parents quite well. Neither is afraid to ask us for what they want for their child. Both have engaged in adult community education during the last couple of years and are therefore in a position to compare this model of education with their own earlier experience of schooling. Both parents would be perceived by their child's school as outspoken. Miller (2000, p. 140) says that 'the respondent will slant their account to fit with what they see as being the interviewer's area of interest and tell their story in a way that they believe will be sensible for the interviewer'. My role as interviewer was to listen to the parents' stories and to try to discover whether, in their opinions, the PICL project had had an impact on them or on their children.

It became obvious during the interviews that each parent had a huge personal agenda about their own schooling. The interview process itself gave each an opportunity to reflect on these experiences. Anderson (1987, p. 100) says, 'If we want to know how women feel about their lives, then we have to allow them to talk about their feelings as well as their activities'. The feelings about school that each parent expressed during the interview indicated the kinds of feelings that entering school buildings might still evoke for each of them today. Until each has some fresh 'first hand experience' of school or education, then that earlier experience continues to be the basis for thoughts, feelings and actions (Easen, Kendall and Shaw, 1992).

Tracy's story about her education (a brief summary)

Tracy enjoyed Junior School but was repeatedly excluded from Senior School for disruptive behaviour. She was not allowed to sit any GCSEs although she says she was 'good at Maths and English'. Tracy feels she has done well, compared with many of her peers, who are 'junkies, alcys and shoplifters'. She says she sees 'a guy who was in my class all the time up the town. It used to be him I used to mess about with – he's an alcy, a junkie – he's a shoplifter'.

Tracy now has a partner, Tommy, and a son, David. She wants David 'to be himself and want to learn', 'to go to College if he wants to so that he gets a better start in life'. She acknowledges that 'if he doesn't want to learn, then nobody is going to force him to'.

Tracy was invited to record what David was doing at home and kept a diary, when he first started nursery. She says that's what 'made me want to go back to learning'. She appreciated understanding what and how David was learning – 'whereas before I wouldn't probably think of . . . well, he's throwing things, now I think "scattering"'. She recognizes his schema.

As an adult, Tracy has begun studying GCSE Maths and English, but has found it difficult along with housework and a part time job. She got a distinction on a computer course but says she 'is not really interested in computers'.

Recently Tracy made the decision that she really wants to work with 'problem children'. She began a College course in the next town, but was told she had missed too much time after the first three weeks (both she and David had been ill). She still feels that things are stacked against her – she is juggling housework, money and caring for David.

Strauss and Corbin (1990, p. 63) say, 'One can count "raw" data, but one can't relate or talk about them easily'. The full transcript of Tracy's story can be analysed by 'conceptualizing the data', that is 'taking apart' each sentence and coding 'each discrete incident, idea or event'. When each incident has been coded in this way, then we can compare phenomena with each other and examine any emerging themes.

After the initial 'open coding' of Tracy's story, a pattern began to emerge. Central to that pattern were Tracy's feelings.

Tracy's story – childhood, lived experience

Table 6.1   Tracy's childhood experience

What was said or done	The feeling invoked	Consequences
Being blamed by teacher for brother's bad behaviour 'They knew where I came from'	Anger	Wanting revenge/ disrupt lessons 'I start messing about.'
Being treated as less important than other children 'I wanted to take exams. I wasn't allowed.'	Feeling like an 'outcast'	Disrupting lessons and exclusion
A couple of teachers 'all right'	Not specified	
Getting caught or being blamed 'I was either kicked out or on report card.'	Numbness	Accepting exclusion as norm
Fighting with teacher over jacket 'She's pulling it and I'm pulling it.'	Loss of control – 'going crazy'/anger 'I started kicking – I don't know what I done.'	Being kicked out
Exaggerating and lying about school events at home 'I'm going to get done if I go home with this little rip.'	Fear of getting into trouble	Excluded/'bored at home' 'It's a loser's game.'
Community placement 'You could get privileges.'	Excitement/ enthusiasm	Enjoyment

There seems to have been a chain of events (Table 6.1), which were repeated during Tracy's secondary education:

A   (Conditions) being treated unfairly.
B   (Phenomenon) feeling angry.
C   (Context) teachers don't help.
D   (Action) being disruptive.
E   (Consequences) being excluded (Strauss and Corbin, 1990, p. 124).

This happened over and over again. Repressed anger, which spilled out when Tracy lost control, seemed justified when we consider what happened from her perspective. Goleman (1996, p. 60) says

Given the roots of anger in the fight wing of the fight-or-flight response, it is no surprise that Zillman finds that a universal trigger for anger is the sense of being endangered. Endangerment can be signaled not just by an outright physical threat but also, as is more often the case, by a symbolic threat to self-esteem or dignity: being treated unjustly or rudely, being insulted or demeaned, being frustrated in pursuing an important goal.

Tracy's mum would always go down to the school 'with the pram' and 'arguing' with the teachers. Tracy and her mum are alike. When her dad became involved, he would only say one word, 'Bed!' Mostly, Tracy was 'grounded' by her parents for her behaviour.

Once, she remembers, she and her mum had to go in front of the governors. 'Me and my mum on two seats in front of about fifteen governors'. On this occasion, Tracy felt that her mum was 'made to feel small' and Tracy 'felt bad' about that. Tracy was asked to leave the room so that her mum could defend her behaviour.

Deep down, Tracy knew that she was capable of studying and passing exams. Sadly, she became resigned to not fulfilling her potential. In the context of the classroom, where she felt 'an outcast', the only way in which she could feel powerful was by disrupting lessons.

According to Robin Hobbs, a psychotherapist running a Pen Green staff training session, one of our basic psychological needs is for excitement or drama (Hobbs, 1998) and school, to Tracy, was generally boring. Children and young people who primarily learn kinaesthetically need firsthand experiences and to experiment in a practical way with various resources in order to sustain interest and to learn (Gardner, 1991). Tracy opted for the '14–16 curriculum project' so that she did not have to sit still and listen in school all day and every day, and could participate in some practical and vocational experiences. This indicates that she recognized that her own learning style required variety.

Recent research on how our brains work show that, broadly speaking, men are 'less likely to endure routine patiently', that 'boys are harder to teach' and that 'disruptive behaviour is not voluntary' (Moir and Moir, 1999, p. 134). The type of behaviour Tracy displayed is more typical of the 'macho culture' of boys (Epstein *et al.*, 1998, p. 82). Often there is a 'class dynamic' to this type of challenging behaviour. The stereotype is that middle-class, neat children work hard and prize academic achievement (Epstein *et al.*, 1998, p. 100). In contrast, working-class children are sporty and can do well but only without appearing to do any work (ibid.).

What follows is Tracy's experience of education, as an adult.

Tracy's story – adulthood, lived experience

Table 6.2   Tracey's adulthood experience

What was said or done	Feeling invoked	Consequences
Having to grow up/pregnant 'Shock! I didn't speak to anyone for six months.'	Fear/uncertainty	Isolation 'I'd walk to the shop for something to do.'
Finding out what was available 'I didn't know all this was here'	Hope/enthusiasm	Start keeping diary '. . . . back into writing and under-standing what he's doing.'
Start studying mathematics and English	Hopeful	Confidence
Took on too much 'I couldn't keep the two going.'	Had a 'downfall'/ despondent	Gave up English
Became too hard 'I started getting stuck on it.'	Despondent	Gave up mathematics 'I know it's there.'
Went on computer course 'Looked through Tresham leaflet – I was stuck in limbo.'	Able	Achieved distinction
Began College course 'I wanted to work with kids in children's homes.'	Hopeful	Setting long-term goal
Being treated like a child 'They forget all them young girls have got no family. We're changing it to this day, that time.'	Powerless/disheartened	Gives up
Being capable/looking after house 'I'll cook the dinners, clean the house . . .'	Proud	Self-respect
Caring what son thinks 'I hope I'm not a down and out.'	Pride	Dignity/ responsibility

As an adult learner, Tracy has had varied experiences (Table 6.2). Clearly, she is keen to learn, but when things become too difficult to sustain, she does not have earlier positive experiences to remind her that she can succeed.

Tracy experiences the system and people within it as 'unfair'. Several times she has begun studying and has not gone as far as she hoped. It seems that her expectation of herself is that she will not succeed. Each time she has to give something up or the obstacles become too great, she says that she is 'disheartened', that she 'knew it would come'. She says that 'school disheartened her'.

This is an analysis of a chain of events that has occurred more than once for Tracy, as an adult:

A   (Conditions) being treated unfairly.
B   (Phenomenon) feeling despondent.
C   (Context) being treated like a child/feeling powerless.
D   (Action) giving up.
E   (Consequences) not achieving goal.

This chain of events does not mean that Tracy has not made progress. It means that she has not yet achieved all the goals she has set herself.

Ironically, Tracy did well on a computer course, which she says 'is not really what I want to do'. She described herself as 'being in limbo' after giving up mathematics and English, and looking for something else to do. She sees using computers as a useful skill, but she would not want to make a career of it.

As time goes on and Tracy gains experience of various courses, she is becoming much clearer about what she wants to do and why she wants to do it. She sees herself working with disadvantaged children in this area of the town, mainly because she has a social conscience and cares about facilities for young people like herself. She feels that there is even less provision for teenagers now than when she was a teenager. She has some good memories of attending a youth club at Pen Green Centre, when the building was much larger. She says that the youth workers 'treated us like adults'.

Tracy says that using the Centre has been significant for her, that she 'started to learn from' when she discovered what was on offer for adults in the Centre.

Tracy's belief in her own ability is still tenuous. With a few more small successes, she might gain confidence and be prepared to fight for her right to an education, which suits her pocket and family commitments.

The second story is Kate's.

Kate's story about her education
(a brief summary)

Kate hated school from the day she started. She would run away from school when she was very young and this continued into her secondary schooling. At first she did not want to be separated from her mum. She says 'I clung on to my mum'. Later on, she was scared that her dad would come in and 'hit a teacher', or embarrass her because he was drunk. She thought 'I've got to get out'. She felt that the teachers would compare her behaviour with his. She thought people would say 'She's just like her dad'.

One teacher was nice to Kate. She felt he was on her 'level'. He handled 'the bad children'. He was the only one to ask 'Did you not like your dad?' Another teacher told Kate that she 'would go nowhere', that she would leave school and 'have a bundle of kids'. Kate thought that teachers were only interested in 'toffee-nosed children'. She says 'They didn't want to listen to me'. She remembers feeling humiliated, 'For swimming you had to walk the whole length of the school with your swimming costume on'.

Kate has a partner and five children, ranging in ages from 5 to 15. When her eldest child began bringing homework home, Kate realized that she 'hadn't a clue what she was talking about'.

Kate decided that she had to do something about getting an education. In between trying various part time and full time factory jobs, she went to college, did a computer course and 'loved it'. She found that most people were there for the same reason and that the students were 'treated like adults'.

Kate has had different experiences with each of her children and is slowly learning to be assertive, rather than 'flying off the handle' when dealing with authority figures. She still does not attend Parents' Evenings or Best Work Assemblies. She says that teachers still have not learnt to tell her anything good about her children.

Kate's full story can be analysed in the following way.

Kate's story – childhood, lived experience

Table 6.3   Kate's childhood experience

What was said or done	The feeling invoked	Consequences/subsequent action
Started school 'I don't want to be here – I don't have to be here'	Fear and anxiety	Ran away 'I'd run out.'
Brothers at home with mum 'Well, they're there with my mum.'	Jealousy	Ran away 'It's horrible.'
Being treated unfairly by teacher 'I got hit in the eye with a golf ball and the teacher told me not to be stupid'	Anger	Ran away
Being put down by teacher 'You'll go nowhere.'	Anger	Ran away
Being ignored 'I needed someone to say "Why are you angry?"'	Anger	Ran away 'I didn't tell the teachers where I was going.'
Being cheeky to teacher 'I'd do things so they'd tell me off and then I'd go.'	Power/they could not stop me	Ran away
Being humiliated '. . . walking the length of the school with your swimming costume on.'	Anger	Ran away
One nice teacher 'I couldn't sit and listen – I might like this and it's too late.'	Fear of liking school	Ran away
Teachers are only interested in snobs 'So let's pay all our attention to them and get them through.'	Anger	Ran away
Step-dad listened 'You're not happy there, are you?'	Valued	Stuck it out

The repeated pattern in Kate's story (Table 6.3) can be analysed in this way:

A (Conditions) being ignored/humiliated.
B (Phenomenon) feeling scared and angry.
C (Context) not fitting in.
D (Action) running away.
E (Consequences) not becoming engaged and therefore no qualifications.

Analysing a repeated pattern in this way stops us from judging Kate's actions and helps us to understand why she developed this strategy. Kate says that the interview process has helped her 'to see things more clearly'.

In Kate's story, the overriding feeling she expressed was one of fear and, therefore, although she was angry, she saw escape or 'flight' as her only possible response to 'endangerment' (Goleman, 1996, p. 60). She says that her mum listened to her and would sometimes go to the school, but that her mum was also scared of the teachers as she could not read or write.

This response became such a fixed pattern that when Kate was tempted to stay and engage with the curriculum, she was fearful that it was too late and that she had missed too much schooling to catch up. She did develop other strategies but they all involved avoidance of school and teachers. When she was older she would phone the school and pretend to be her mum, saying 'Kate won't be in today – she's got really bad period pains'. Sometimes she would 'hide in a cupboard at lunchtime'.

Some form of 'escaping' continued to be her only strategy. When her mother remarried and Kate had a step-father who listened and understood that she did not like school, his advice was to 'stick it out'.

Kate felt angry when she was a child but feels her anger was ignored. As an adult, Kate is more in touch with her anger and has a deep commitment to supporting each of her children (Table 6.4). Her own experience, as a child, seems to have given her an insight into how things can be handled differently. Her eldest daughter did run away from school, but her teachers listened to her version of events and were able to sort out a bullying problem. Kate still feels sad that she herself was not listened to when she was a child. Being an advocate for her children has enabled Kate to learn to 'talk things through' and not 'fly off the handle'. Kate identifies closely with one of her children, who is currently excluded from primary school. She

Kate's story – adulthood, lived experience

Table 6.4   Kate's adulthood experience

What was said/done subsequent action	The feeling invoked	Consequences/
Inability to help with homework 'I hadn't a clue.'	Inadequacy 'It was so simple.'	Tackle problem of no education
Goes to college 'Other people are like me – they haven't got a clue either.'	Confidence	Achieving goal
Child's teacher not listening to him 'He's got my nature – when he goes on one . . .'	Anger 'I'd be straight down.'	Losing control
Coming to research – being contradicted 'People are brought up in different ways.'	Inadequacy/anger 'My upbringing was terrible.'	Stopped going
Child's teacher putting child down 'A teacher called her "stupid" in front of other pupils	Anger	Thinking things through 'I wrote down everything she told me and showed the Head of the school.'
Being assertive 'I was calm on the outside.'	Powerful	Being listened to by authority figures
Child's photos displayed in research base '. . . they are watching what he's doing.'	Pride 'That's my boy – I'd tell people.'	Observing child and recognizing his ability 'When he's built that circle thing, that's really nice.'

says, 'He's not a bad kid – he just seems to get the blame. He's well known for getting into trouble and now he is punished for really petty things'.

Kate's experience of going to college has been positive. Kate thinks that the reason for her more positive experience at college is because 'the people are the same as me. They haven't a clue either. There are no smart arses'. Also she appreciated 'having a laugh and joke with the tutors'.

Kate is planning to go back to college later this year to study for an NVQ in Playwork. Her decision to go back to college has been a difficult one to make. She still has ambivalent feelings about the system. She knows it will be a struggle but believes that she can achieve and says 'It'll be great to stick my finger up to people who didn't think I could do it'.

The adults' learning processes

Tracy has learnt to control her anger but still feels that the system is unfair. She seems resigned to not yet achieving her personal goals.

Kate no longer runs away from education. Even though she was not listened to as a child, she is able to listen to her children and to ensure that their teachers know how they feel. Most of Kate's energy, up to now, has been directed towards sorting out interpersonal and behavioural issues at her children's schools. Recently one of her children was called 'stupid' by a teacher in front of other pupils. Kate not only listened to her child, but wrote down everything that happened, including the child's feelings. Kate contacted the school, discussed the issue with the head, who wanted no further action on Kate's part. Kate was not satisfied with this and insisted on an interview with the head and the teacher concerned. Kate was able to confront the teacher with evidence of how he had made her child feel.

We hope that by engaging parents in the PICL project, and encouraging them to discuss their children's emotional and intellectual development, many of them will feel confident enough to discuss their children's all round development with other professionals.

We want parents to be involved in discussing their children's education. Listening to Tracy's and Kate's stories can help us to be more aware of some of the barriers to coming into nursery or school for a minority of parents.

The barriers to becoming involved from the parents' perspectives

Personal and interpersonal barriers

What follows are the personal feelings expressed by Tracy and Kate that might be evoked whenever either of them enters a school environment and might therefore prevent them from feeling at ease in such an environment:

- feelings of anger, fear and anxiety;

- not fitting in;
- feeling undervalued;
- feeling numb;
- isolation;
- tendency to run away/avoid authority; and
- feelings of inadequacy.

Some of these feelings were evoked originally because of the way Tracy and Kate were treated by other people in the environment, usually teachers. Their feelings about teachers and other authority figures might also be reinforced by family attitudes. These attitudes towards other people are described as interpersonal.

Teachers in school are often perceived by pupils as very powerful (Pollard, 1996). The memories and experiences that Tracy and Kate describe, depict the majority of teachers as people who act unfairly, blame certain children for everything that goes wrong, only like and help 'snobs' or hard-working children, humiliate and ignore children. Both parents acknowledge that there are exceptions.

These pupils react by telling lies, exaggerating, dramatizing, running away from school and disrupting lessons. They feel justified in behaving in this way.

The role of Tracy and Kate's parents was crucial. Neither set of parents was able to convince their child that attending school and working hard has long-term benefits. Both sets of parents felt uncomfortable in the school environment. They did not view teachers as being like them and therefore they were 'unconfident' in dealing with them assertively.

Organizations are usually run by powerful people or people who have succeeded in attaining a position of authority. Often they are run to suit the majority and this may exclude minorities. We are aware of 'institutional racism', that is when organizations have rules or structures that prevent minority ethnic groups from joining (Arnold, 1967). Schools sometimes have rules that prevent some children from having an equal opportunity to attend, for example, an expensive uniform, which is obligatory. These sorts of barriers are structural.

Structural barriers

The overstructuring of the curriculum seemed to be a barrier to Tracy becoming engaged at school. Silly practices like 'walking the whole length of the school in your swimming costume' made Kate feel humiliated and therefore less motivated to participate.

There seemed to be a lack of information for pupils and their parents about courses. Tracy did not seem to realise that if she chose the 14–16 Curriculum Project, she could not even sit her GCSEs. Tracy's and Kate's parents were not knowledgeable about curriculum issues. Were any efforts made by the schools to communicate with them about curriculum matters? Did they attend open evenings? If not, how would they know what was available for their children? Were open evenings easily accessible?

When Tracy's jacket was torn in a tussle with a teacher, that was a huge issue for her. She felt she had to exaggerate what had happened so that she was not blamed for spoiling her new jacket. In this instance, her mum went straight down to the school to complain. Replacing the jacket was a serious concern in Tracey's household. Money is often tight and prevents some children from taking part in extracurricular activities, which might engage them more than the regular curriculum.

Strategies we have used to engage Tracy and Kate and other parents at Pen Green

Bearing in mind the sorts of barriers that may have prevented parents from participating in education in the past, we have developed the following strategies.

To overcome barriers connected to personal feelings

Often parents are anxious and lack confidence. If we accept them and their children and genuinely like them, then parents will begin to loosen up. We must always be scrupulously fair and sometimes this involves explaining our decisions and policies to parents. They have a right to know how decisions are made. Whenever possible, we can involve them in the decision-making process. We always try listen to complaints and apologize if we are in the wrong.

It is important to acknowledge feelings, the parent's and their child's. Often something quite small makes parents angry. If their child goes home in wet socks, they are entitled to feel cross with us for not noticing. We can apologize and make sure we check socks in future.

We offer one-to-one support if parents are shy or lack confidence in a group situation. Sometimes they might want to express an anxiety or we can spend time discussing the key concepts and how they relate to their child's progress.

Sometimes parents need convincing that they and their child have potential. We closely observe children and this is invaluable information to pass on to parents on a daily basis if possible. This can alert the parent to specific things to watch out for at home and to share with us.

We often reflect back to parents the major role we see them playing in their child's development and learning. For example, when Tracy kept a diary, David was seeing her writing each day and that increased his knowledge of communication. Soon after, he became interested in numbers and letters.

To overcome barriers connected to attitudes to other people

We want parents to get to know us as individuals and we want to get to know each of them as an individual. The only way to do this is to spend time together. During the two weeks that parents spend settling their children into nursery, we have a golden opportunity to chat informally with them and to get to know a bit about them. It is only fair to tell them about ourselves and our families, if they are interested.

Once we know something about their life, we can try to engage them in coming to a group. Some parents might be ready to study or meet with other parents to discuss their children. Others just want to get a job or have some time to themselves. We have high expectations of parents and we know that the majority want more information about how children learn and how they can help them.

As time goes on, there are many other ways that we can build our relationships with parents. We can invite them out on a trip with their child, to a social event in the Centre or ask them to show visitors around the Centre. This acknowledges that they are our equals, that we enjoy and value time spent together and that they have gained knowledge as a user of the services, which they can share with visitors.

Although we are working hard to build relationships, we try not to patronize parents. Being honest with them is important, for example, Kate did not agree with her son playing with dolls in the nursery. We discussed this issue on several occasions, each airing our views freely. We agreed to differ on this point.

Parents who are not confident about writing often like using a video camera. Often fathers are interested in technology for themselves and for their children. Tracy's partner became very engaged in observing David when they borrowed the nursery video camera.

Overcoming barriers to do with the rules and structure of the organization

When the organization is inflexible and unresponsive it is not helpful. We find it is a good rule of thumb to think through the reasons for having rules. Our family room at Pen Green used to be a room where parents could smoke. Four years ago, after nearly two years of discussion and consultation between parents and staff, we made it a no smoking area. This was agreed mainly because of the children's health. However, we still feel that it is important to have a small smoking area if we are to welcome all parents into the Centre. Most of the study and support groups have a no smoking policy, which is negotiated when a group begins. However, we can be flexible and have a 'smoke break' halfway through a meeting if that suits the parents.

Coming out of the organization and making visits to children's homes on a routine basis is something that staff and parents seem to appreciate. Tracy says, 'When Lorna (family worker) came, David was taking her up to his bedroom. He thought everyone lived at nursery. I said "Lorna's got a house. Lorna's got children" '.

When we evaluate our work, it is important to ask parents how things have been for them. New ideas stimulate our thinking and often these come from parents. We are constantly listening out for what parents want and trying to offer it. Recently some Portuguese families moved into the area from the Algarve and they now have English as a second language classes with crèche facilities for their children at the centre.

How Tracy and Kate got involved in the research and development project

Tracy

- Tracy became involved in attending a session on schemas. This was when David would still not separate from her, so he came along too and one of the workers played with him during the session.
- Tracy kept a diary of what David became involved in at home for six months of David's two years at nursery. Over the same six months Tracy attended a weekly study group.
- Tracy and Tommy borrowed the nursery video camera twice. Tracy says Tommy 'is right into technology'. Shortly after this, both parents came to a science and technology evening in the nursery. We had set up the television and video camera, computers and our

CD-ROM, which illustrates how children learn through exploring schemas. Tommy found it fascinating.

- Again, both parents came to an evening study group, when the focus was on boys' achievement.
- Each year we run an assertiveness programme for the children who are due to start school. We call it 'Learning to be Strong'. We begin by having a parents' meeting to discuss the programme with parents. Tracy and Tommy attended this meeting.
- Tracy went on a day trip to the Science Museum in London with other parents and staff and also attended a family group meeting at nursery.

Both parents came to a meeting about reports for school. During the interview, Tracy said that the following ways of being involved were significant for her. Keeping a diary was a turning point for Tracy. She said that that was 'when she started to learn'. She was 'back into writing and understanding what he's doing'. She also enjoyed attending the study group. Sometimes she would say outrageous things, but we all knew and liked her and there was a spirit of fun in the group. Tracy remembers borrowing the video camera, although it was Tommy who did most of the filming. 'David would carry on with what he was doing when Tommy filmed him.' The 'Learning to be Strong' parents' meeting was important and helpful to both parents. The discussion about bullying helped Tracy and Tommy to make a difficult decision about which school to choose for David. The 'Learning to be Strong' sessions for David were 'well worth doing'. When David first started nursery, the family had just moved back to the area and he was quite insecure. His family worker and parents put together a book containing photographs of people who were important to him. This 'family' book was significant for David. It helped him to settle at nursery. Tracy says, 'He used to walk about carrying his book'.

Kate's involvement in the project

It was when Kate's youngest child started nursery that the PICL project began. Kate did not see herself as the type of parent who becomes involved in Centre activities. She says 'I'm not the type – Pen Greeny. I haven't been to baby massage or to this group or that group'. She also expressed her ambivalence about not having been involved when her older children were nursery age. 'Why should I do it for him when I didn't do it for Carl? I've never done things like that before.' Despite her resistance to involvement, Kate became involved in the following ways.

- Kate attended a study group in the evening twice. She said during the interview that she finally came 'to see what it was like' because we kept 'nagging and nagging' and she thought 'they *do* want me to come'. She found the first meeting 'interesting' but the next one was 'rubbish'. Her main reason for not enjoying the second meeting was that 'whatever I said, somebody always contradicted me'. (Kate is referring to other parents and staff disagreeing with her.) Some contentious issues were discussed to do with smacking and telling children to hit back when other children hit them. Given her history of 'being ignored' and 'not being listened to', she possibly found mild disagreement quite threatening to her self-esteem.
- Kate also became involved in discussing her son's portfolio individually with Cath. She agreed to take some photos of her son playing at home, after describing to us the complex play that he became involved in with his cars and using the bottom of the wardrobe in his bedroom. The photos never materialized and when asked why, Kate said she tore them up because her house looked messy.
- Kate attended a meeting about reports for school.

Kate said that the following things about nursery were significant for her. Having a full time place in nursery for her little boy, Mark, who had been 'a poorly baby'. Kate became interested in what Mark could do 'at his age'. She says, 'I was shocked at what he could do. He was doing different things to what Carl was doing'. Kate was proud of Mark's photos displayed in the research base. She said 'I didn't think I'd ever see my kids' photos up anywhere here'. She added 'Oh my God – people are going to come in here and see my son on the wall'.

We can learn a great deal from listening to these parents. It is easy to sit back and judge parents without knowing very much about their passionate concerns. We can measure the effectiveness of our service by how hard we work to reach the hard to reach parents. The final comment is from Kate (about her children), 'I'd want them to do something like stay on at school and to think "I *can* do this" '.

What we need to remember is that:

- we want all parents to become involved in discussing their child's education; and
- we may need to develop very different strategies to engage parents who have had poor experiences of education and schooling.

7

The Impact on Parents' Lives

Annette Cummings

This chapter gives an account of how Annette, formerly a parent at Pen Green and now a teacher in the nursery initially got involved in the research project. It also describes three nursery parents different experiences of being involved in a study group over a period of one to three years.

Annette's Account

As a family worker at Pen Green I am now in my second year of co-leading a research and development study group which focuses on the parents' involvement in their children's learning. As a group leader I have found the group absorbing, thought provoking and enlightening. It has been wonderful to watch the parents grow in confidence and knowledge as the year progresses. It is also fascinating listening to the parents' views and comments on how their children engage in play at home. Each parent brings to the group a wealth of knowledge of their own child which helps to provide a more holistic approach to the child when it comes to planning provision for the nursery (see Chapter 8). Throughout the two years that I have run the group, I have become very interested in the way that the parents' involvement with their childrens' learning project has had a knock-on effect in relation to the parents' own personal growth and development.

Getting involved in my own children's learning

One of the reasons that I really enjoy co-leading the Parents' Involvement in their Children's Learning group is because it was getting involved with my own children's learning that pushed me to go back to university to do a postgraduate Teachers' Certificate in Education. When my eldest child started at the Pen Green nursery in 1993 the research and development at the work at the Centre was in its early days. Even then, all the nursery parents had a chance to go to a training session on schemas which was led by Tina Bruce, an education consultant and author of several books on early childhood education.

At this time, in my life, I knew nothing about schemas but I did know that the things Alexandria was doing at home were driving me mad. Alexandria, who was aged 3 at the time, had a favourite game which was 'Hide and Seek'. She used to get inside the duvet and do the poppers up or get in between the curtain lining. She always wanted to dress up and put make-up on. Meanwhile, my youngest child, Olivia, who was aged 16 months, used to empty tins out of the cupboard, in the kitchen, and put them into her pram and wheel them around the house. Between both children I thought I would go crazy.

I went along to a child development session, at the Pen Green Centre, when Alexandria was attending the nursery, and I found the whole thing mind-blowing. Everything fell into place. Alexandria was displaying a typical 'envelopment' behaviour and Olivia was a 'transporter'. I was hooked, it all seemed so simple, the schema training helped me to understand my children better and also helped me to make extra provision at home to help them extend their play.

When Olivia showed signs of 'envelopment' schema I just took it in my stride. I knew exactly how to support her in her play and bought her 'Polly Pockets' which would incorporate both schemas (envelopment and transporting). Alexandria is now 9 years old and is still a strong enveloper. She still likes to dress up and put make-up on. When she entered a fancy dress competition recently she transformed herself into the Statue of Liberty!

Olivia is still displaying her cluster of schemas which include envelopment and transporting. On a recent holiday to Minorca Olivia wanted to pack her own hand luggage. When we reached our apartment she disappeared into the bedroom and reappeared five minutes later. I though nothing of it until I went to hang the clothes up in the wardrobe. When I opened the wardrobe door there were 37 teddy bears staring at me. Olivia could not stop laughing, she thought it was very funny that nobody knew she had transported them all the way to Minorca from her room at home.

The parents that I work with (Figure 7.1), in the research group, have had similar experiences. For example:

* Louise has two children, Sean and James, and is married to Scott. Sean started nursery in 1996 and left to go to school in 1998 when James, his younger brother, started using the nursery. Both children have had the benefit of attending nursery for two full years,

which seems to us, at Pen Green, to be ideal. Louise has been attending the PICL research group for four years.

- Eloise is married to Dave, they have two children, Becky and Jessica. Eloise has been going to the PICL group every week for the last three years. Becky spent a year at the nursery and has now moved on to primary school and Jessica is full time in the nursery and will be there for two years in all.
- Dave is married to Tracey and they have two children, Lorin and Ross. Both parents attend the PICL group. Lorin has moved on to school and Ross is in the nursery. Dave has been going to the PICL group for 18 months.

Starting the group

All new parents, both mothers and fathers, are encouraged, by their family worker, to join a research study group when their child starts nursery. They are normally introduced to the programme on an initial home visit well before the child comes into the nursery. As a teacher in the nursery I always talk to the parents to explain how invaluable it is for us to have information on what their child is doing at home and I explain how that information is used in the nursery. I also explain that learning about why your child does certain things can help in terms of what you provide for them in the home. It can also increase your understanding about the way that children think. Parents are very interested in what their children are learning and

Figure 7.1 Parents in the research group: Eloise and Dave with Becky and Jessica

most of our parents have some link with the research project either through attending the PICL group, keeping a diary, or through coming along to the key concept training sessions in the first term or sometimes by attending a family group meeting.

Some parents find going to a group difficult to handle and sometimes it is the thought of their own literacy skills that come to the forefront. Their anxieties about writing often date back to their own experiences of schooling. This literacy issue is sensibly dealt with by the staff so that most parents can feel comfortable about attending. Staff explain that, although some parents in the group will want to keep diaries, there is no need to write anything down if parents are reluctant writers. All parents can discuss their children's interests and development orally in a supportive small group setting. Sometimes parents have low self-esteem, so gentle encouragement is needed to get them to attend the group. I always tell the parents that joining the group is also a good way to make new friends because as parents they all have at least one thing in common, their children.

The parents' reactions on joining the group

The parents' reactions on joining the group were as follows.

Louise's feelings on starting the group

Sean was 3 and started nursery and I decided to become involved in the PICL group. I had already been at the centre doing lots of other parent groups and I really enjoyed the centre, it gave me something to do during the day and somewhere where I could learn. So I started the PICL group and I really enjoyed it, it just broadened my horizons as to what Sean was doing.

Sean was really boisterous as a toddler, he was very physical. He was always into climbing, running around, hiding and running away. I had to run a lot, after him, and be behind him a lot of the time as he was always doing dangerous things. James, my other little one, does exactly the same. I found Sean quite hard. Being your first child I always felt as if wherever I looked it was always Sean that was, you know, mucking about, as they say, or running about or throwing things. He used to throw everything. He used to be quite rough with other children, which was really hard. When Sean started nursery, and I had the opportunity to join the PICL group and learn something about why he was doing these things, I thought 'brilliant'. It was an ideal opportunity to give him everything I could, you know, from learning myself. The PICL group really opened my eyes as to why Sean was doing things.

Going to the Group itself was about making new friendships and also just about being able to get things off your chest and being reassured as to why the children were doing things rather than bottling everything up, talking to people who understood as well, you know, the nursery staff who run the group, could help you out.

Eloise's feelings on joining the group

My family worker, at the time, was Annette. She talked me into going, she talked about these wonderful diaries that we would keep and video tapes and all sorts of things but I wasn't that keen, I must admit, the thought of keeping a diary didn't appeal to me and I just thought that my writing would not be as good as everybody else's. I was placing myself low down, I didn't have the confidence but I went to the first meeting and that was it. The staff were wonderful, they made you feel as if you wanted to go back, they gave you the confidence, they didn't pull you down if you said something that was utterly stupid.

When I first thought about going I was cringing inside and the night before was like 'Oh god, I've got to go to this group and somebody might speak to me. What if I go red and what if I say the wrong thing?' I thought I just didn't want to go, but I went, 'cause I thought that Annette might kill me if I hadn't gone! Nobody sort of laughed at you, whatever you said was good, you know, it just gave me the confidence to go back. If I had hated it I would never have gone back.

Dave's feelings about starting the group

I started with the PICL group a month after Ross started nursery. He has been coming to nursery for roughly 18 months and I have been doing the PICL Group for much the same time. I went along mainly to get involved with knowing why Ross was doing certain things, because when our daughter was coming up to 7, she came through the nursery and there were things she did, playing at home, that would drive me mad. My wife, Tracey, was involved with the nursery anyway, coming to baby groups and groups with Lauren before, she would say 'she's doing this because of this and this is her schema' and I didn't know anything about what she was going on about.

I was interested to come along when Ross came to nursery because I was now permanent night shift, whereas before I used to work a double day shift, 6–2 or 2–10, so I couldn't get involved. I wanted to come along and find out why Ross was doing certain things and how he could be encouraged. We found that Lauren was always encouraged, with drawing and painting and writing and even with simple maths, at nursery. Now, at school, she is in the top group in the class, she reads really well, better than some children I know who are a lot older and she writes and spells words that my boss, at work, would struggle with. She's really doing very, very well so I was encouraged to come along to these things, to the group, to find out how I could help Ross in the same way as Lauren had benefited.

Also, going to this group, I have managed to find out about things that my child does that I was not particularly pleased with or happy about. We used to be a bit wary of Ross bouncing around, jumping off the furniture, now, rather than tell him off all the time, we realize the only thing we can do is make what he does safer so my sister-in-law brought him a trampoline for his birthday. He used it a lot, rather than the furniture, which is encouraging. He bounced around on the trampoline until he became, not bored with it, but he'd bounced enough and now it's in the playhouse in the garden and if they're out in the garden in the summer he'll bounce on it again.

Getting to know about patterns in children's play

All the parents using the groups have made huge discoveries about the patterns in their children's play. Because they had all attended introductory sessions on schemas they began to use Piagetian language with confidence to describe and account for their children's behaviour.

Finding out about schemas

Louise

When I first went to the group it was just brilliant knowing why he was doing things, especially the throwing, 'cause he used to throw everything and obviously that was his trajectory schema. They told me that he was going on to learn about area and everything to do with mathematics and things and I was thinking 'WOW' and it took a little while to sink in really but then as I went to the group I learnt more and more why he was doing things at nursery and it was relatively easy to see what he was doing at home. Sean used to flood my bathroom, he liked to see the water overflowing; before I was getting really angry, because it was, like, so-called naughty things he was doing. Obviously, it still is a bit naughty sometimes 'cause you don't want your bathroom soaked or whatever but why he was doing it was because he was learning. I used to try and think of alternative things for him to do which wasn't wrecking my house and being dangerous. One thing he used to love was glass, he loved to see it smashed which was really out of order. So I took him to the bottle bank, you know, hoping it would satisfy his need, but it wasn't enough, he still used to go on about glass. So at the PICL group, which was a lovely group, we talked about it. You felt as if you could go in and tell the group what they were doing, getting worries off your chest, and you'd be reassured why he was doing things. So then the staff at the PICL group suggested I get some ice cubes, so in the summer I used to freeze loads of ice, let him go out in the garden with a big bucket and a hammer and he loved the banging and he used to smash all the ice everywhere, all along the path and that, and it seemed to satisfy his need and then he sort of went on to something else.

I found the group really helped me in finding ideas for things for Sean to do that were interesting and safe.

Eloise
I enjoyed coming to the group it made me understand what Becky was doing. I mean, she was driving me nuts, she was filling nappy sacks, Jessica was a baby at the time and Becky was leaving them all over the house. If we wanted anything it was in a nappy sack somewhere knotted up. That sort of opened my eyes and I found other things more suitable than the plastic nappy sacks she was using, like paper bags and envelopes, and it's just gone on from there.

Becky's envelopment schema was so strong you could leave her and the house could have fell down and she wouldn't have cared. I mean, with Becky, what she was doing at nursery, she has taken with her to school and she is doing very, very well with language and literacy I mean her language is brilliant.

Dave
I'd spoken to Tina Bruce on a number of occasions on study days and I've always found what she had to say really interesting because you look at your children and you don't realize the hidden things, their ways of thinking. Before the schema training I would have spent all this money on toys that he wouldn't play with whereas now I know I would have saved myself a lot of money and I've bought him boxes, some wooden boxes, anything to put things in and move them about because he's into this enclosure schema. We've learnt that you don't have to spend a lot of money on expensive toys that they're not going to play with. At Christmas this year, through the PICL group, knowing that Ross was into dressing up (envelopment schema), we bought him a dressing up Buzz Lightyear wings and mask and helmet. A lot of our friends spent hundreds of pounds on their children but with Ross he had nearly everything he wanted. He was really excited about everything he got and he plays with everything, not just like Christmas Day and Boxing Day and

it's all forgotten, he's still playing with everything we bought him now and I think we'd have struggled to spend £50 on him this Christmas. I've gained a lot of new learning talking with Tina and finding out how she gets her ideas and things and I've borrowed a book by Tina, from Trevor, the Head of Centre, and I've been taking it to work with me and it's fascinating, it's really good.

Ross has been interested in Sellotaping things, connecting things together with Sellotape, tying things, making up parcels, he's forever bringing us things in paper stuck with Sellotape and saying 'I've brought you a present', so one of the staff suggested we buy him a Sellotape dispenser. Because he'd got little hands he can't peel the Sellotape off the roll and they've got one at nursery and he knows how to use it so we bought him a big Sellotape dispenser, some paper, pens and bits for Christmas. It was the best present we could have bought him at the time, this Sellotape dispenser, and the Sellotape was all over the house but whereas a lot of parents would have been annoyed at the Sellotape stuck to the doors and wrapped around the chair legs and things, we know why he does it. It's made our life a lot calmer.

The diaries

Although I was involved with a research group when my daughter, Olivia, was at nursery the one thing I regret is not keeping a diary of her everyday play. I do feel sad about it but I make sure that I tell all new parents about how I feel in the hope that it will encourage them to keep their diaries up. At that time there was no support group for parents at Pen Green so I felt isolated and insecure about what to write and I did not make the effort. Nowadays the subject of what to write in the diary always crops up and is covered during the session when the co-leader and myself talk through the key concepts in child development, which parents have been introduced to in their initial training session. Parents learn to apply these key concept to their children's play. For instance, parents soon realize it's worth writing things down or videoing their child when they are deeply involved and knowing about the Involvement Scale really seems to help.

During these sessions the question of poor literacy skills and low self-esteem often rears its ugly head. Horrible tales from school are told and many parents report how cutting remarks from teachers have had a detrimental and lasting effect on their self-esteem and belief in themselves as learners. Again, reassurance is what is needed. I have always explained that when I read their diaries I'm not interested in checking their spelling or the grammar: I'm just interested in the content and I want to find out what the children have been doing at home so I can feed that information back into the nursery planning. Once all the initial problems have been sorted out, and the group settles into a routine, it is a privilege to listen to what the parents have to say about their children, and how they have been playing with them at their home. Parents love to write about their children even if they are not sure what their play has been about, and when they come into the group they like to talk about what their child has been doing even if they find their children's behaviour challenging.

Louise on keeping diaries

It's brilliant, I really enjoy writing things down and even now go back sometimes to Sean's and flick through, you can't believe some of the things you said, you forget so quickly. It's really good looking back at what you've said, and at the group you use your diary to sort of help prompt you then in the group as to what they've been up to and why they were doing things. This is what the group is all about, sharing what your children are doing.

Eloise on diaries

Well, I have and I haven't kept them. Becky's was pretty good, Jessica's I've not been so good this year, I don't know why, I just can't get into it. Maybe it's because Jessica's schemas aren't so clear. Becky had one schema and she was easy to write about whereas Jessica has a cluster of schemas. One day she's got one schema and the next week she's doing something else so I don't know. It is nice to have a diary and look back at it and I wish I'd carried on with Becky when she went to school and I haven't. With Jessica, I will. Now Becky's left nursery she's got her diary up in her wardrobe and she's really proud of it, and her portfolio, she loves it, she's just so proud of it and I am too.

Feeling confident in a group

Once a group is up and running and the boundaries have been set it is amazing how quickly the group feels at ease. Boundaries around confidentiality are very important to make it safe for parents to open up and share experiences. It is very rewarding to see the group help each other, not only in terms of their children's learning but also through developing friendships and gaining personal support. Last year, in the group that I ran, the parents supported each other through two marital separations, two births, a death in the family and an older child leaving home. As the trust builds up within the group, between parents and staff, there are certain personal issues that parents may feel the need to share. These needs must be addressed not only to ensure the well-being of the parent but also because it gives the other group members an idea of where that parent and their child are 'coming from'. For example, a sudden change in a child's behaviour might be because his mum and dad have separated and the child does not want to see his dad. Once the scenario has been discussed within the group it gives some context to what the parent has written about the child. More often than not there is usually a group member who has been through a similar situation and they can offer help with different strategies to cope through these difficult times.

Parents openly discuss and celebrate their children's play but will also talk freely about things that they are not happy about, especially if it is a child's challenging behaviour. The staff and other parents provide a listening ear and sometimes offer advice on how to deal with particular issues. Parents become confident to speak out in these relatively small groups. They become better at listening to other parents and feel able to offer appropriate advice to each other.

Louise on being part of a group

I suppose the big thing I got out of the group was that what the boys' were up to was OK. It boosted my confidence as a parent just knowing it was OK. I used to feel, a lot of the time, that Sean was the only one in the whole world that was doing these things and I got to realize that he wasn't and everybody else was able to share their anxieties as parents and it made me feel a whole lot better. Because a lot of the time, outside of the group, I'm really honest about what they do and sometimes I used to think that maybe I said too much. I sometimes felt as if other parents wouldn't say the things I said, they only said all the good things and that used to make me feel even worse. So going to the research group was about sharing and everybody in the group is the same, they used to share their anxieties and it just helped us to understand that it was OK.

Eloise's feelings about the group

I felt confident, at the group, you knew that you weren't going to be judged for smacking them for really being naughty. Like when Jessica, who was going through a cutting-up stage, got all my letters off the door mat and sat and cut them all up. I was cross and I had to tell her off because there was my TV Licence and everything else in that pile so I had to say that this was not right, I mean even though she was doing her trajectory schema. I had to tell her that that was wrong, you know, she couldn't do things like that, she had to ask before she cut important things like the mail up.

There are days when your children really wind you up and I felt confident enough to say 'Yes, I'm having a really bad day'. I felt OK about it because everything you say in the group is in confidence anyway. We covered *everything* in the group, I mean a couple of times we just sat and talked, it's not every week it's about your diary. If there was something bothering somebody, staff would sense that, then we would discuss that, if the person felt comfortable about it, which I quite enjoyed as well. Sometimes it was nice to get something off your chest. I mean, there was one session we were talking about ourselves and a couple of them were in tears, you know they had got something off their chest.

Sometimes it was nice to hear other people were going through the same thing as you and you didn't know or realize about it. I mean, I didn't get very far at school and I never liked school, and I want things to be different for my children. I could have died at school and nobody would have known if I was there. I sat at the back of the class and I think the PICL group has helped me, not to push my children to where they don't want to do anything but to go with them and if they're having a bad day I say 'Well fine, tomorrow's another day' and we can start again and we'll try again and we'll go as far as we can, we can do the best we can. You know, I speak to Becky's teacher every single day whether she likes it or not and if Becky comes out of school and there's something bothering her I go back now whereas before if I hadn't gone to the PICL group I would have put my head down and said 'Never mind', now I go back up and whether Becky's got the story wrong or right I go and discuss it there and then. I do not keep it or hold on to it anymore I just go and get it sorted out which I would never have done before. So it has given me the confidence to do that, before I would have died rather than go up and speak to the teachers.

Dave on being part of the group

If there's something that we don't particularly like him doing at home or something I am worrying about, I felt I could talk about it in the group. For instance Ross had a dummy and I used to say, he was nearly 4 at the time, and he still had this dummy stuck in his mouth. I mean, I criticize people for saying I don't like my son playing with prams or I don't like my son playing with dolls or dressing up and all this and I criticize people for that, yet I could see myself doing much the same thing and saying the same things about his dummy. I used to talk about it at the PICL group, I used to come to it and say 'Look, what am I going to do about it, this dummy?' and lots of the parents were saying, you know, that they had to leave it for Santa, one of them said that her son buried it in the garden and things like that. We went on holiday and for the whole fortnight Ross had it stuck in his mouth and I used to get really worried thinking 'Oh what's he gonna to do, he's got all these dummies and people are gonna think look at the size of that kid with that dummy'. The week after we came home I was at the point of thinking 'Oh, no' I was gonna hide them or throw them all out and just tell him they'd gone but one night he was going to bed, he had his dummy and he just said to me, 'I don't like the taste of this'. I said, 'Well, we've only got two or three, try this one I'll run it under the tap'. He replied, 'No I don't like the taste of that one'. I said, 'We haven't got any more'. He replied, 'I don't want one then'. He put these three dummies on his chest of drawers in the bedroom and went to bed, that was the end of it, he never had them again and afterwards I kept thinking all this fuss I've made and people would have been thinking 'Oh my God, here he goes again about this bloody dummy' but all this fuss I'd made, at the end of the day, he was the one who instigated finishing it and we've learnt, a lot of the time, from the group, a lot of the parents had said that he'll give it up when he wants to and I was thinking 'When will that be?' but I didn't mind going to the PICL group and saying 'Look I'm really concerned about this' even though, that in a way, I was being very similar to the ones who say I don't like him playing with prams, or I don't like doing this, I could see that I was along those lines but I didn't mind saying it because I felt really strongly about it.

What do parents get from the group for themselves?

When I was involved with a research project as a parent I found the whole experience enlightening. It made me feel that I understood my children a lot better and I did not get cross with them so easily. It made me look at what they were interested in and I knew that if I wanted half an hour of time for myself, the best thing was to go to the junk market, buy Alexandria some more dressing up clothes (envelopment schema) and Olivia a 'Polly Pocket' (envelopment/transporting schema) and then I would have time to sit and read a book or do the crossword because they would be busy. Apart from helping me with my children, the research project helped me to find a sense of direction and make a career change – from working in the fashion business into teaching. So off I went to De Montfort University and took a Postgraduate Certificate of Education course. I passed the course with a Distinction but the proudest moment for me was when I stood in front of my year group and explained to them what schemas were all about, using my own children's patterns of play as examples. From the conversations I have with the parents who attend PICL group and the three parents I have interviewed for this chapter, the general consensus is that the group is definitely a confidence builder and in some cases, mine included, it can lead to a major career change. The majority of parents who have been involved with the PICL group go on to other courses such as the City and Guilds accredited Crèche Worker Course that is run at Pen Green. Others go on to take a National Vocational Qualification in Childcare at the Centre (Pen Green is an NVQ Assessment Centre). Some parents co-lead groups at the Centre and these parents can become paid workers through the local further education college if they have a basic qualification in training adult learners (City and Guilds 9282).

The PICL group also helps parents feel strong enough to make decisions about their children and to challenge the people who have all the power and control if their child is unhappy. I have found that parents who have had negative school experience, who have had no support from their own parents, really do want to make a difference to their own children's education and support them all the way through their school careers. They want to be advocates for their children. Parents feel less stress when they understand why their children are playing in certain ways. With knowledge about child development concepts they can try to turn problematic situations around so that they can become positive learning experiences. Coming to the group every week has helped the parents get to know their children better and has helped them to build a better relationship with each other. Parents become committed group members and friendships grow in the group.

Parents have also told me how their children love them coming to the group. The children see their parents write in their diaries and this encourages the children to be interested in writing and early literacy. The children also love the fact that their parents spend time in the nursery talking to staff at the beginning and end of each day; finding out what the children do at nursery that is the same or different from home is critically important for parents. They are also very anxious to know who their children are playing with.

Parents enjoy watching their children on video in the group. It is a good chance for them to see what their children are engaged in at nursery. Also parents like to show off the videoing skills they have gained by coming to the training session on videoing children which is offered to all parents. This session is led by a professional video maker, Penny Lawrence, who works on the non-fiction parts of the Teletubby series.

Parents become schema spotters and look for the involvement signals. Parents genuinely feel respected as their child's first educator. They see staff keeping records and planning for individual children and know that staff are deeply concerned to support each child's learning.

Louise – what it's meant to be part of the group

Coming to the group really helped my confidence in wanting to learn more about the children and now I've gone on to run a group myself to do with babies, it's called 'Growing Together' and it focuses on under nursery age children where parents can come and sort of learn, from a really early age, why children are doing things. I really enjoy doing it because it's sort of an extension of me being involved with the PICL group as a parent, now I'm helping to run this one and it's really gone well. I found being in the role of the teacher strange at first because you feel a bit, well you've always been to groups as a parent, but I want them to learn what I've learnt through the group. I'm really enthusiastic about, you know, letting them see what I've learnt through the group, how it's opened my eyes as to why my children are doing the things they do, and you know just finding that understanding. The group's helped my confidence. My boys come first and being their advocate, going to school and being able to talk to their teacher has been important.

When Sean started school there was a bit of a problem. I sort of had a word with the teacher about it and I wouldn't let it go. It was to do with his baseline assessment. To me, I knew exactly why Sean hadn't done very well in baseline because it takes Sean a few months, the person he is, to settle into change, to feel comfortable, to do his best. So I went in and explained that to the teacher, now, you know, after a couple of months he's coming out with flying colours. So you know I've followed it through with Sean and the group has made me a lot more confident to speak to teachers. Like I say, when I had Sean I really wanted to learn about children's development because you have a baby and it's a whole new world I didn't really know anything about how children learn. I wanted to do something for myself so I did my Diploma in Child Day Care by correspondence then I went on to do the Confident Parent Confident Children Open University group at Pen Green. Then I went on to do the PICL group and since then it's really taken off. I really enjoy working with children. I now work in a play group at the sports centre. James goes to school in September so I think that's a turning point for myself. I always thought I'd like to be at home with the children when they're small but when they do go to school then it's time for me. I'm halfway knowing what I'd like to do and, you know, I was just thinking about whether to do my NVQ when James goes to school in September.

Eloise – what's it's meant to me and the future

I'm seriously thinking about the Crèche Workers' course at Pen Green once Jessica's in school because once she's in school I haven't got any more excuses. I do want to do the Crèche Workers' course but something deep down inside says 'Oh God' I'll have to write and do essays and that's what's holding me back. I could have done it this year but I used Jessica as an excuse so next year I'm not going to have Jessica so I'll see how I go. I might need a good kick up the backside to make me do it. Hopefully the group will springboard me on to something else. I'd say I feel more confident with people, I have to push myself more because my husband's away from home but if David was at home all the time I don't know how I would be. You know, there's only one person that can help you and that's yourself really in the end. The group made me understand my children more, it's given me the confidence to give them a push if they need it and yet not to push them too hard. I don't get cross so quickly with them now because if they're doing something, like Jessica cutting up the mail, even though I had to tell her what that was wrong I don't scream and shout like I would have done. I will miss the group, it's not a trudge, it's not like 'Oh God, it's Tuesday afternoon and I've got to go to the PICL group'. I feel good that it's Tuesday. I'm going to miss it, it's part of my life now, it's been three years and I've made friends. I help now at the Messy Play Group and mixing with parents. I have to speak to other people, it's something I make myself do. I have to push myself and I'm going to start a Mums and Tots Group over at the school, with Connie on a Monday morning starting next month so that will be meeting new parents. It's a shame really that there's not the same thing at school – where you could carry it on, but I suppose with the limited resources they have they're just not able to do it.

Dave – what the group's meant to me and the future

The group helped me as a parent. I think it's great because I work permanent night shifts and it's horrible to say but it's more like a social event. I mean you come and chat with other parents and it's always good to come. I love it, I love coming to the group, we have a chat and a laugh. I've learnt so much more about my children and I've learnt how to encourage them to learn through playing and what they're getting out of what they do. Apart from my own children, I've never had that much experience with younger children so I started helping at the nursery; through my involvement with the PICL group I've become more involved with Pen Green than my wife is. She's done her A-Level English here but I've also done parent interviews for the Sure Start project and I've interviewed to appoint new staff. I've personally gained a lot from it, I mean I sort of found out now I've got other career opportunities really as well as developing various skills like visiting other people in their houses and doing interviews. I've had training, I've helped out with interviews for staff at Pen Green as well, which I never have been asked to do anywhere really other than at work and I also found that, in my opinion, my input has been valued and that's something that helps everybody's self esteem and personal development. One of the senior members of staff asked if I'd ever considered working with children as a career which I hadn't. I'd never really thought it was a viable career opportunity really until I sort of looked into it and then thought maybe I could do the NVQ through gaining experience working with the Pen Green nursery children.

What next?

Louise

After Louise left school at 16 she went straight into an office, carrying out general administrative duties and was amazed that she lasted in the job for eight years! When Sean was born it was time for Louise to move on. She did O-level psychology and typing at the local college and eventually got a job at the local sports centre working on the reception and then moving on to working in the crèche.

At this point in her life Sean had started attending nursery at Pen Green. Louise with her new baby James continued to use the baby groups at Pen Green and then embarked on the Open University group 'Confident Parents, Confident Children'. Attending all these groups and courses made Louise want to go on and gain more knowledge and insights into her children's learning. It was at this point that she joined the PICL group. From there her career has snowballed. She has had paid employment from the Centre working in the kitchen and in the office. She is now a course leader of the 'Growing Together' group paid for by the local college. This group is a research group concerned with supporting parents with babies and toddlers who want to understand more about their infant's learning and development.

Since Sean has moved to primary school Louise has been a volunteer in the classroom and her husband Scott has recently become a school governor. Louise is now completing her NVQ level 3 and works as a member of supply staff in the nursery.

Eloise

After spending time in the school system, Eloise left school at the age of 16 with one O-level in Religious Studies and some CSEs. She had very low self-esteem and felt as though the system had 'let her down'. She was enrolled into a work experience programme in a clothes shop and absolutely hated it. Moving on she got a job at a local supermarket and when the yearly review of all employees began Eloise was taken by two senior members of staff into a room and was told that she had to practise speaking into a mirror to boost her self-confidence. At this point she left the firm!

She was offered a year's work on the Community Industry Programme for school leavers and she was placed in a local infant school as a classroom assistant. Eloise loved this job but had to leave when the year was up.

For the next 11 years she worked in two factories and was employed as a packer. She then left to have her first child, Becky. Eloise began going to a group called 'Messy Play' for under threes, and then moved onto join the PICL group. She now has paid employment in the Centre, working as a kitchen assistant, and as a volunteer. She helps to run the Messy Play session, supporting other parents and their children.

Dave

Dave left school at 17 and went on to a building site. He then worked as a painter and decorator for two years before moving into warehouse management.

Dave is on the road to a new career through coming to the Centre and joining different groups. He has now enrolled onto the Wider Opportunities Programme, a European Social Fund Employment Scheme run by staff at the centre. He is attending a course called 'Introduction to Childcare', which is a preparation course for the NVQ in Childcare.

Dave works as a volunteer in the Pen Green nursery on a Thursday afternoon and now has paid work supporting a child with additional needs in the nursery every afternoon at storytime.

Last year Dave got involved with the Sure Start programme's Parent Led Needs Assessment (Pen Green Research Base Report, 2000), interviewing parents on a range of issues. This was paid work and he has been approached to do follow-up interviews this summer.

Although Dave still works night shifts as a warehouse manager his new career in childcare could not be further from the career he planned when he left school.

Benefits for parents and children

As a teacher and as a parent I have seen the benefits of being involved with the research programme. Returning to university had an impact on my whole family. When my children used to see me preparing work for the next day they would say, 'It must be easy at university – all you have to do is write!' Both children have told me they want to go to university. Alexandria wants to be an architect and Olivia wants to be a children's writer.

The parents that I interviewed for this chapter, Louise, Eloise and Dave, have all told me how coming to the group has made a huge impact on their children's lives. Sean, after a difficult transition into school, has settled down and is doing well. Becky has told Eloise that she wants to be a teacher and Lorin has a high reading age for her age.

Their younger children James, Jessica and Ross are all decision-makers at nursery and all have strong clusters of schemas which are supported at home by their parents and in nursery by the staff. All their children have a strong sense of security and a belief in themselves which makes them confident, autonomous learners, risk-takers, and likely to succeed in school.

> Parents and carers of young children in whatever family configuration or circumstance thus have an absolutely vital role in education for they are the most significant reference point with regard to children's identity, learning stance, the scaffolding of understanding of learning outcomes.
>
> (Pollard, 1996, p. 307).

8

Dialogue and Documentation: Sharing Information and Developing a Rich Curriculum

Margy Whalley and Marcus Dennison

In this chapter, we describe:

- the conditions under which *a dialogue* can develop between parents and nursery staff and nursery staff and other early childhood professionals;
- the way in which information about children's learning at home and at nursery can be shared, and common understandings negotiated through *'The Pen Green Learning Loop'*; and
- the development of a range of *documentation* and its use as a critical tool for communication with parents, and for staff development.

Reflective practice

Practice needs theory and theory needs practice, just like a fish needs clean water. Practice apart from critical reflection, which illuminates the theory embedded in practice, cannot help our understanding. Revealing the theory embedded in practice undoubtedly helps the subject of practice to understand practice by reflecting and improving on it.

(Freire, 1996, p. 108)

Staff at Pen Green are deeply concerned with *praxis*. Praxis means reflective practice or, in the language of early years, 'learning by doing', then spending time thinking about what you have done and making links between theory and practice. In Colin Fletcher's words (1999, p. 159) praxis is about 'revising and refuting action on the basis of reflection'. What this means for us at Pen Green is that we have begun the process of converting our competence as early years practitioners into theory which can be understood and then discussed with parents and other early childhood educators.

Charles Handy, the management guru, describes those of us in the field of education as 'conceptually impoverished' (Handy, quoted in Scott 1996, p. 4); without the conceptual skills to resolve the dilemmas we now face. He argues that 'it is no good doing things right – using technical and human skills – if they are not the right things to do'. Our view is that early years education is the one phase of education which is conceptually rich; child development concepts underpin all our day to day practice. What has been lacking in the past in the foundation stage is a *shared* language with which to articulate our shared understandings (Drummond, 1989; Whalley, 1994). We have made reference to this shared language in several chapters because it seems to us to be a central issue for early years educators.

Relatively few settings have appropriate levels of non-contact time for staff to reflect on their practice and learn to dialogue with each other, the children, the parents and the wider community. Staff at Pen Green, however, have always had non-contact time and our practice is underpinned by a strong theoretical framework. Many of the Pen Green staff team, like early years educators in other settings, first became interested in working with young children because of a passion for social justice and commitment to children's rights. Staff were aware that critical reflection was the key to improving practice and that we had to constantly improve our own understanding if we were to honour the needs of the children. Korczak (writing in the 1940s) identifies the all important emotional dimension to this learning process. 'Thanks to theory I know, thanks to practice, I feel. Theory enriches intellect, practice deepens feelings, trains the will' (Korczak, quoted in Bettleheim, 1990).

Developing a dialogue

Freire (1970, p. 71) tells us that there is a series of steps which have to be taken before participants, in this case staff and parents, can engage in critical thinking. What we need to do is to:

- perceive our own ignorance and give up the idea that we are the exclusive owners of truth and knowledge;
- identify with others and recognize the fact that 'naming the world' is not the task of an élite;
- value the contribution of others and listen to them with humility, respecting the particular view of the world held by different people;
- get in touch with how much we need other people and have no fear of being displaced; and
- be humble; have faith in others and believe in their strengths.

Throughout the 1990s, Pen Green nursery staff worked hard to develop this way of engaging in critical thinking in collaboration with parents and other professional colleagues.

Recognizing our own ignorance

Some of the staff were parents themselves but not all; some lived locally but others travelled in a distance of 25 miles; none of us knew enough about the context in which the children lived. Often the assumptions we made about children and families were wildly out of line with reality. Through regular home visiting on the parents' terms and at times that suited their family life style, staff became more knowledgeable about the children and their families. With this information, we could celebrate the richness and diversity of the children's experiences and at the same time become more aware of the pressures children and families were experiencing.

Identifying with parents

Staff quickly learnt to 'start from where people were'; parents who were desperately trying to hold down two jobs and struggling with childcare did not want to be perceived as uncooperative if they could not turn up for daytime or evening meetings at the nursery. However, without exception they valued the time staff spent in visiting them at home. When staff sent videotapes home of the children playing and learning in nursery, parents were willing to reciprocate in kind. Often these tapes would contain just a short video clip of a child deeply involved in an interesting learning experience; sometimes the child would be engaged in behaviour which staff did not understand. Staff would add to the vignette of the child's activity a small video clip of themselves asking the parents whether they had seen the child involved in this kind of play at home. Parents would almost always offer a response. Whilst they accepted our desire to understand more about the children's cognitive concerns, they also reminded us that significant social events were also relevant and gave us information about the important life events that were taking place. When staff asked parents if they would be interviewed about their own educational experiences they willingly shared their memories of struggling to make themselves heard in the school system. They made it clear to us that they wanted something more and something better for their children.

Valuing parents' contribution

Many parents did attend meetings or got involved in study groups and these were always run in a way that respected the different needs of families. Parents arriving at 7 p.m., having just come off a shift, needed a relaxed atmosphere and refreshments, but they often also wanted a well-prepared and focused discussion. In these groups, we had to establish a dialectic where contradictions could be tolerated, important problems could be posed and important questions answered (Allman, 1983, p. 111). Parents were given opportunities to explore their own uncertainties; they were not force fed with content and knowledge.

Mutual need

Nursery staff were very clear that they needed the information that parents held about the children's learning at home. Without this information, we could not provide the kind of supportive, stimulating and challenging curriculum that the nursery children deserved.

> 'The roles of professional experience and parents' everyday experience are seen as complementary but equally important. The former constitutes a 'public' (and generalised) form of theory about child development, whilst the latter represents a 'personal theory' about the development of a particular child. An interaction between the two 'theories' or ways of explaining a child's actions may produce an enriched understanding as a basis for both to act in relation to the child. *Only through the combination of both types of information could a broad and accurate picture be built up of a child's developmental process'.*
>
> (Easen, Kendall and Shaw, 1992, p. 285, emphasis added)

Recognizing parents' key role as the child's first and most consistent educators did not leave staff feeling de-skilled or supplanted. Parents and staff began to see themselves as co-educators, co-constructing an appropriate curriculum to meet the cognitive and affective needs of every child.

Recognizing parents' strengths

Staff were constantly having to revisit the theory and review their own practice in the light of information proffered by the parents and our detailed observations of the children. At times we struggled to understand what a child was doing and were unable to support a child's deep interest in a particular learning experience. Then we were very dependent on parents for additional insights. Chris Athey describes the same process in the Froebel project, 'because the search was for fundamental patterns of thought, parents became increasingly involved, to the point of fascination in educational issues that, in the past, might have been thought to be the sole province of professionals' (Athey, 1990, p. 207).

The Pen Green loop

In describing the Pen Green Loop (see Figure 8.1), we are trying to address what Chris Athey calls the 3Ps of early childhood educators: 'parents, participating with professionals within an articulated pedagogical approach' (Athey, 1990, p. 56). The learning loop is a dynamic process whereby all the important adults in a child's life give each other feedback on what seems to be centrally important to the child, and how and what they are learning in the home and in the nursery.

Parent-led observations and feedback to staff (see Figure 8.1, sequence 1–4)

Parents had, in the main, attended at least two training sessions on the key child development concepts that inform our practice in the nursery.

They were also offered a training session on how to use the camcorder and how to make effective video vignettes of their children playing and learning at a deep level. These parents went on to make detailed observations of their children at home and shared these observations with the nursery staff either verbally or in written form at the start of the nursery session, or during one of the study groups. In these study groups, parents were given time to reflect on what their children had been doing, they shared ideas with other parents and received information from staff about what was interesting the children in the nursery. Like Louise in Chapter 7, parents often relished the opportunity to share their anxiety about apparently naughty behaviour (Athey, 1990, p. 207). They were often reassured when their children's behaviour was reframed as consistent and predictable. Staff were able to relate the children's play to the child development concepts that parents had studied, and parents were also able to attribute new significance to what their children were doing (Athey, 1990).

Some of these parents borrowed the nursery camcorder or used their own, and made video vignettes of their children playing in the

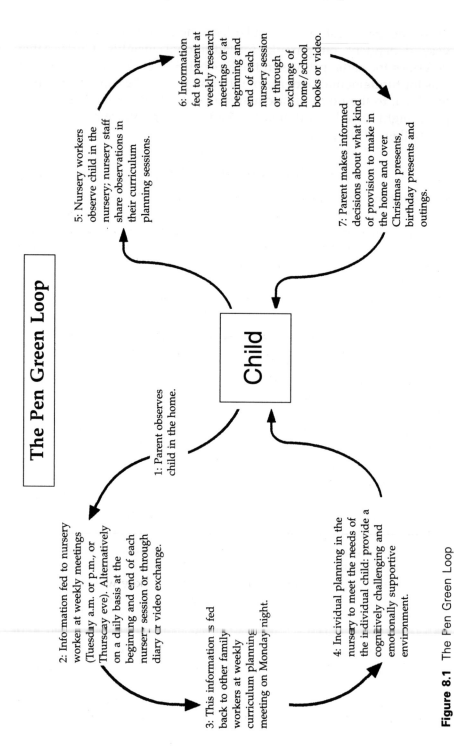

The Pen Green Loop

1: Parent observes child in the home.

2: Information fed to nursery worker at weekly meetings (Tuesday a.m. or p.m., or Thursday eve). Alternatively on a daily basis at the beginning and end of each nursery session or through diary or video exchange.

3: This information is fed back to other family workers at weekly curriculum planning meeting on Monday night.

4: Individual planning in the nursery to meet the needs of the individual child: provide a cognitively challenging and emotionally supportive environment.

5: Nursery workers observe child in the nursery; nursery staff share observations in their curriculum planning sessions.

6: Information fed to parent at weekly research meetings or at beginning and end of each nursery session or through exchange of home/school books or video.

7: Parent makes informed decisions about what kind of provision to make in the home and over Christmas presents, birthday presents and outings.

Child

Figure 8.1 The Pen Green Loop

home setting. Nursery staff were given some additional time out of nursery to copy these diary entries so that the diaries could be retained by parents. Staff also jotted down verbal information offered by the parents directly on to the nursery planning sheet, or into each child's 'celebration of achievement' file. Research staff and nursery staff who ran the study groups made it a priority to watch videos brought in from home and to make notes on a special data sheet which they subsequently entered into the child's file. Alternatively, they might share the information brought from home with the child's key worker at a weekly curriculum planning session which all the nursery staff attend. In these staff planning sessions, individual staff would present their observations of particular children; other staff would share any other observational evidence gathered from home or from nursery. The whole staff group would then begin to familiarize themselves with the children's interests and identify their cognitive constants, and any emerging patterns in their play. Staff would also share their knowledge about the children's emotional well being and developing social relationships within the nursery.

On the basis of informed observations in the nursery (Bruce, 1997, p. 67) which were fleshed out by observations in the home setting, staff could then begin to plan to meet the needs of individual children or groups of children.

Staff led observations and feedback to parents (see Figure 8.1, sequence 5–7)

In the same way that parents observe their own particular children at home, staff have a system for observing the children in the nursery. Every day two children are flagged up as 'target children' (systematically over a four- to six-week period, every child in the nursery is targeted) and all staff, students and parent helpers make sure that they fill in observational records on these children if they come into 'their areas' in the nursery. These observations provide the evidence base for planning for each child. It is the child's key worker's responsibility at the end of each session to collect all the observations that have been made that day. If staff are on leave, colleagues will put their observations in the children's files or wait and swap observations at the Monday evening nursery planning session which last from 4.30 p.m. until 6.00 p.m. At this planning session, nursery staff are encouraged to challenge each other's thinking and begin to make links between theory and practice.

Nursery staff also receive regular supervision from a senior member of staff. They can use these supervision sessions to discuss issues about particular children in more depth. All the observations that staff make, and the decisions they arrive at about planning for the children in nursery, are shared with the parents. Information can be passed on to parents in the following ways:

- through daily chats at the beginning or end of a session;
- through home-school books or videos that nursery staff have made; and
- through the research study group which runs in the morning, afternoon and the evening each week.

Parents use the information that staff share with them to make informed decisions about how to extend the provision that is available at home to support their child's learning; what sort of outings they might go on and what kinds of Christmas or birthday presents they might select.

Freire reflects on how knowledge emerges through just this kind of dialogue. In this way, we can 'reconsider through the considerations of others, our own considerations' (Freire, 1970, p. 61)

To demonstrate how effective this sort of exchange of information can be we next consider a worked example of the learning loop.

Parents and staff as co-educators: the learning loop

Alice and the conveyor belt

Every week we plan to support and extend children's learning in our nursery and we often start with their questions. Alice's questions were all about how conveyor belts worked. However, we need to put her questions in some kind of context.

Chelsea, Alice's friend, had travelled up to Scotland in December and saw her luggage 'disappear' down a conveyor belt. She wanted to know where her luggage went to. She came back to nursery and shared her experience with her friends and the nursery staff. In January, the nursery staff made a number of experimental conveyor belts to explain the concept to Chelsea. Although it was Alice, not Chelsea, who became deeply involved. At the end of January, Alice and her mother went with a small group of parents and children from the nursery to visit the Launchpad at the Science Museum. She found the complex conveyor belt particularly exciting. Chris Athey (1990) comments on the importance of widening children's experience beyond the school walls, to feed their schemas and to generate new learning. Susan Greenfield also reflects the same viewpoint, 'experience is a key factor in shaping the micro-circuiting of the brain' (Greenfield, 1997, p. 122).

Home/nursery dialogue

Lesley, Alice's mother, is aware that at 3 years 10 months, Alice has a cluster of schemas. The schemas which have been particularly important to Alice for several weeks are enclosure, envelopment and rotation.

Enclosure is concerned with enclosing oneself, an object or space.
Envelopment is concerned with covering or surrounding oneself, an object or a space.
Rotation is concerned with turning, twisting, or rolling oneself or objects in the environment around (Arnold, 1997a).

Lesley regularly keeps a diary of what Alice does at home and brings it into the research study group every Tuesday afternoon. These particular diary entries show some interesting examples of envelopment:

16 Oct: Alice found a balloon in the drawer. After I had blown it up for her, she spent a little while chasing it. I then caught her spreading William's nappy cream all over the balloon!! Aarrgh!!

17 Oct: Alice was drawing on a little note pad. As she finished with each page, she ripped it off the pad and wrapped up a fridge magnet in each piece of paper.

20 Jan: I bought her a sellotape dispenser for Christmas and she now uses up rolls and rolls of sellotape . . . She wrapped sellotape around her little brother in his baby walker.

Lesley's family worker also runs the study group so he makes copies of these diary entries and shares the information with other staff and puts her comments into Alice's file.

Problem-solving in nursery

Over several months Alice spent time experimenting with the conveyor belt. She was actively engaged in problem-solving. It took her some time to understand that by pulling the belt underneath, from right to left, she could make objects move from left to right, so that they fell with a satisfying clunk, into a metal container.

Alice has a hypothesis that all the objects she puts on the belt will move along the belt in the same way, and then drop off the end. When she put a ball on the conveyor belt, she was initially intrigued.

However, after trying two or three times to make the ball behave in the same way as the flat objects, she rejects it. She chooses to discard the ball because it presents her with contradictory evidence. She was excited by her own theory and she continued to experiment with other objects which behaved in a way that confirmed her hypothesis. Wynne Harlen (1982) writes of children's need to develop a 'false hypothesis'. Alice's false hypothesis was that all the objects she placed on the conveyor belt would behave in the same way. As she becomes more experienced she will modify her hypothesis.

In the research study group Alice's key worker, Marcus, shows Lesley what Alice has been doing in nursery (Figure 8.2). Both Lesley and her partner are fascinated by the conveyor belt experiment and are impressed by Alice's concentration and disposition to learn. In both the study group and the staff meeting we share ideas about just what Alice is learning.

What is Alice learning?

It seemed to nursery staff that Alice was developing an understanding of some important mathematical and physical concepts, 'learning mathematics or science is not so much learning facts as learning ways of thinking' (Lee and Das Gupta, 1995, p. 219).

The concepts she was investigating were concerned with:

- forces and motion;
- friction and gravity; and
- surface area.

At the research study group

Lesley continues to attend the research study group which is held on a Tuesday afternoon. Each week she shares her diary entries with the staff who run the group and with other parents. The members of staff running the group keep a record of the group discussion that relates to Alice on a 'research feedback' form (Figure 8.3) which is then put into Alice's celebration of achievement file for her family worker to read

This particular study group spent some time discussing how parents could best support children's envelopment schema and when it was necessary to set some boundaries around inappropriate behaviour. Lesley's comment was that 'my relationship with Alice has become much more engaged – I feel I am on her level and much more in tune with her play. Finding out about schemas has helped to put me one step ahead!" Chris Athey (1990) does make the point that to 'identify a schema is not necessarily to love it'. Lesley was very clear

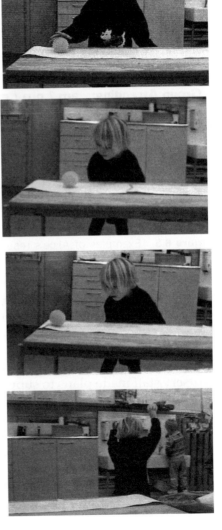

Figure 8.2 Alice and the conveyor belt learning sequence.

Research Feedback Form
Name of Child: Alice
Name of Parent: Lesley
Group Attending: am / pm / evening 28th October

Issues Raised

Lesley has noticed that Alice is wrapping up the door handles with sellotape. She is also wrapping up (enveloping) the televison tuner in tea towels or tissues. Lesley says she will let her wrap up all the family xmas presents. Alice woke at 6am and tried to envelop her whole face with lipstick and blusher (she doesn't enjoy face paints). She also wrapped plasters round all her fingers.

Research Feedback Form
Name of Child: Alice
Name of Parent: Lesley
Group Attending: am / pm / evening 28th October

Issues Raised:

Lesley noticed that Alice was winding her lipstick out until it was fully distended and then put the top on it – squelching the lipstick inside. At this point Lesley banned further use of the lipstick. Alice also tried to cover her whole face with eye shadow but it didn't work (envelopment). Alice gave her mother a pretend 'feather' which was a straw enveloped with paper and Sellotape.

Figure 8.3   Examples of Alice's research feedback forms.

that she had set an appropriate boundary on Alice's use of her make up bag and David, Alice's father, was happy to offer Alice an alternative as we can see from the extracts from the research feedback in Figure 8.4.

Planning to support and extend Alice's learning

Nursery staff made plans to support and extend Alice's learning using a PLOD (possible lines of direction) chart. Central to the nursery planning were the narrative and video observations parents and staff had made of Alice's cognitive constants at home and at nursery.

Alice is learning at a deep level; at nursery we want to build on what she *can* do and encourage her to develop an interest in what excites her. The PLOD chart which we have developed (Bartholomew and Bruce, 1993, p. 45) helps us to integrate our observations of the

Research Feedback Form
Name of Child: Alice
Name of Parent: Lesley
Group Attending: am / pm / evening 18th November

Issues Raised:
Alice had enveloped an egg box in paper and wound it round with sellotape and some raffle tickets all in one big parcel. She used up the rest of the roll of sellotape. Lesley asked her to go to the loo before she went out and Alice came downstairs and commented, 'the loo roll looks just like the sellotape'. Alice enveloped her dolls' faces with chalk like she had her own in nursery.

David, her dad, brought her two children's lipsticks and she put the purple one on top of the pink one and said she had made a new colour. Lesley let her use some tiny paint pallets at home and she mixed colours. Sometimes she envelops her little brother, William, in the beanbag!

Research Feedback Form
Name of Child: Alice
Name of Parent: Lesley
Group Attending: am / pm / evening 25th November

Issues Raised:
Lesley reported that Alice had run into nursery saying 'my daddy's really usta-ful'. She wasn't sure is she meant beautiful or useless!

Alice had made a dog lead with links and attached it to William (18 months) and encouraged him to 'walk' like a dog. She sometimes says 'the dog done it' if she spills her drink. This morning Alice was cutting out a boat and a house and colouring them in and she had to stick them in Lesley's research diary.

Figure 8.4   Extracts from research feedback.

children's interests, their schemas, and at the same time make links with the early learning goals. At the centre of the PLOD (Figure 8.5) are the names of several children who all share Alice's interests. Chris Athey (1990, p. 30) makes the point that 'unreflective child centred-ness has led to the false belief that every child needs a unique edu-cational programme. Constructivist teachers know that many children share similar cognitive concerns'.

By 4 years of age Alice was still experimenting with the conveyor

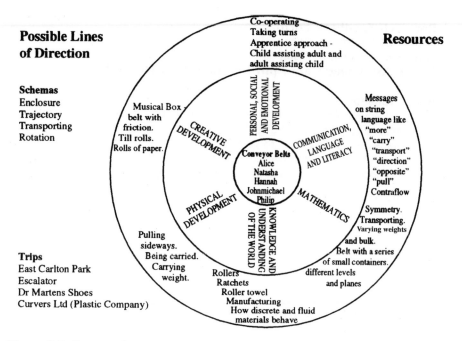

Figure 8.5 Extracts from research feedback

belt but by now the nursery provision not only included the improvised 'belts' that staff had made out of paper, but also a manufactured
conveyor belt. This conveyor belt when placed in the sandpit offered
Alice and other nursery children a new range of possible lines of
direction. Alice's parents' deep commitment to her learning and their
partnership with the nursery staff has made it possible for us to offer
Alice a stimulating and challenging nursery environment.

Documentation

Pedagogical documentation as defined by Gunilla Dahlberg
(Dahlberg, Moss and Pence, 1999) makes it possible for:

- the child to revisit and reflect on what she has done, and in this
  way to make her learning an active process;
- nursery staff to enter into a dialogue, and communicate in action
  with the child and her parents;
- the nursery staff group to open up the nursery so that it becomes
  a public space, an arena for discussing critical questions and for
  reflection;

- the nursery staff to develop materials as a basis for reconstructing pedagogical practice, for reflective dialogue, negotiation and challenge and to connect theory and practice; and
- nursery staff to problematize their practice and planning and open it up to critical analysis.

Dahlberg reflects on the long tradition of pedagogical documentation in Sweden and in Italy. She differentiates between the reflexive problematizing approach of Kohler in Sweden and Rinaldi in Reggio Emilia, and the approach of traditionalists who see observing children 'as being about mapping some universal and objective social reality' (Dahlberg, Mass and Peace, 1999, p. 145). Dahlberg defines pedagogical documentation as critically different from 'child observation', 'as we understand it, the purpose of child observation is to assess children's psychological development in relation to already pre-determined categories produced from developmental psychology and which define what the normal child should be doing at a particular age' (ibid., p. 146).

Susan Isaacs at the Malting House school in the 1930s, who pioneered the use of observation and whose studies have influenced many early years practitioners in the United Kingdom, *was* concerned with building and substantiating generalizable theories about children's learning and development. However, she was also concerned with differences in the behaviour between children and in finding out more about the particular interests of individual children (Drummond, 1993, p. 49). She was also deeply interested in knowing more about children's rich emotional lives and showed a remarkable acceptance and understanding of children's negative feelings. There is nothing sanitized about Isaac's descriptions of experimentation inside and outside the classroom (Isaacs, 1936). The children in her school were interested in life, death and bringing things back to life. Compare her notes in 1930 with those of the Pen Green nursery staff in 2000.

Susan Isaacs' observations in 1930

13.7.25: Some of the children called out that the rabbit was dying. They found it in the summerhouse, hardly able to move. They were very sorry and talked much about it. They shut it up in the hutch and gave it warm milk.

14.7.25: The rabbit had died in the night. Dan found it and said, 'it's dead – its tummy does not move up and down now'. Paul said, 'my daddy says that if we put it into water, it will get alive again'. Mrs I said, 'shall we do so and see?' They put it into a bath of water. Some of them said, 'it's alive, because it's moving'. This was a circular movement, due to the currents in the water. Mrs I therefore put in a small stick which also moved round and round, and they agreed that the stick was not alive. They then suggested that they should bury the rabbit, and all helped to dig a hole and bury it.

15.7.25: Frank and Duncan talked of digging the rabbit up – but Frank said, 'it's not there – it's gone up to the sky'. They began to dig but tired of it and ran off to something else. Later they came back and dug again. Duncan, however, said, 'don't bother – it's gone – it's up in the sky', and gave up digging. Mrs I therefore said, 'shall we see if it's there?' and also dug. They found the rabbit, and were very interested to see it still there.

(Isaacs, 1936, pp. 182–3)

Pen Green staff observations in 2000

15.2.2000: We are reading 'The Dog that Dug'. On one page there is a picture of a skeleton of a dinosaur. James asks if the dinosaur has been eaten. I explain that it died a long time ago and that the skin and flesh has rotted away. James asks 'when we are dead why are we always dead?' I explain how things stop working inside us and don't start again. He says, 'My grandpa Alex is dead'. I ask him if he is sad. 'No' he says and then 'a little bit' and then 'my Grandma is sad'. I say that she is probably missing his Grandpa's company. James asks 'Who is going to sleep with her now?' I say that I don't know. He asks 'When you get old you die', and 'am I getting older?'. He continues, 'when I'm big I'll be old. Are you old?' he asks me, I say that we get older every day. James asks, 'am I getting older?'

Drummond (1993, p. 50) makes the point that Isaacs's work celebrating, as it does, the children's individual emotional and intellectual lives also provides a salutory warning for early childhood educators, 'if we choose to see only those aspects of learning of which we approve, we will lose the opportunity to see more of the picture, to learn more about learning . . . there is always more to learn, and more to see' (ibid.). It would be very easy as adults to focus our observations on what interests *us*, on the aesthetically pleasing for example rather than on those things which are of deep concern to young children.

Penny Lawrence, in our video training sessions for parents and staff, reminded us that whilst the camera provides a window into the child's world, we see that world through the lens of our values and beliefs, and we focus the camera on what *we* consider to be worth observing.

Whilst there are some significant differences between the documentation that takes place in Sweden and in Reggio Emilia and that which takes place at Pen Green, there are also some similarities. The time-honoured tradition of observation which underpins the work at Pen Green derives from the studies undertaken by such baby biographers as Darwin, Piaget and Navarra (Bruce, 1997, p. 10) and the observational approach pioneered by Susan Isaacs in the 1930s. At Pen Green we focus on the children's learning process. We observe what children are doing and saying and we then interpret and analyse what we see using currently available theory (Bruce, 1997, p. 67). Subsequently we share ideas with colleagues and the children's parents, develop plans to support and extend the children's learning. We document this whole process working in collaboration with the children's primary carers.

James's interest in death, dying, beheading and whether executioners were 'bad men' was supported and extended by the nursery staff. He was offered storybooks that enhanced his understanding such as *Grandfather Cherry Blossom* and *Kintaro the Nature Boy*. His strong trajectory schema which we had observed since he was 2 and 3 years old had led to an interest and developing competence in using the saws on the work bench and in making swords. James was supported and extended by the introduction of a special kitchen saw so that he could behead a dead fish and examine its bone structure. He was fascinated by the concept of transformation of state and tried to make the decapitated fish come alive again in a bowl of water. He also reflected to his key worker that if we left the fish in water for a long time then it would come alive and if that did not work we could put the fish in the lake and it would come alive. Much of James's learning about cause and effect was through hypothesizing, and verbal discussion, practical investigation and reflection. James showed little interest in representing his experience, although at one point he briefly wallowed in red paint. The formal record of the experience was through the documentation of the staff and his mother, that is, video clips and notes in James's file. However, the learning process was deep and sustained over several weeks, and we have included both home video of James and his mother, Louise, and nursery video in our new training pack.

Like Gunilla Dahlberg in Sweden and Carlina Rinaldi in Italy, staff at Pen Green have begun to see how making our observations, dialogue, analysis and planning more explicit can be useful for staff, parents, children and the wider community. 'Documentation offers the teacher a unique opportunity to listen again, see again, and therefore revisit indirectly and with others, the events and processes in which he or she was co-protagonist, directly or indirectly. This revisiting with colleagues helps create common meaning and values' (Edwards, Gandini and Forman, 1988, pp. 121–2).

Portfolios of children's learning

At Pen Green we now produce *portfolios of the children's learning*. These portfolios are critical if we are to develop and improve our practice for the following reasons:

- The portfolios are useful for children because they can revisit and reflect on what they have done; we call this metacognition.
- They are useful for nursery staff because they form the basis for discussion between children and their parents; they also encourage reflection and make it possible for staff to reconstruct their pedagogical practice. Staff can dialogue with colleagues, problematize their practice, and make links between theory and practice.
- Documentation is also important for parents because when their children's work is opened up for discussion in this way parents can ask critical questions and reflect on what their child is doing at nursery.
- These portfolios also honour the contribution that parents are making as their child's first educators. The dialogue we enter into with parents, children and the wider community is not cosy. We often need to share strong views and challenge each other's ways of thinking. Parents are passionately committed to supporting their children's learning and nursery staff work with parents as equal, active and responsible partners.

All documentation at Pen Green is developed through a dialogue with the children's parents. Becky's portfolio shows how the information is collected, how observations are shared and how parents and staff work together to support and extend Becky's learning. The final document is a celebration of Becky's achievements which she takes home and which she can share with her teacher when she moves on to primary school.

Becky's portfolio

BECKY STARTS NURSERY
When Becky came into nursery in September 1997, her mum reported, '*Becky can spend hours hanging outdoor clothes, moving and folding them – then repeating the process all over again.*'

After being in nursery for a couple of weeks, she is enveloping herself and others in stickers. Her mum reports, '*Plain white stickers are not good enough, they must be coloured ones . . . she draws circles, cuts them out and puts them on top of each other.*'

Becky seems to have an envelopment schema.

DEFINITION OF SCHEMA
'*Schemas are patterns of linked behaviours which the child can generalise and use in a whole variety of different situations. It is best to think of schemas as being a cluster of pieces which fit together.*' Bruce, 1997.

Becky's Cluster of Schemas
Envelopment – covering or surrounding oneself, an object or a space.

Enclosure – enclosing oneself, an object or space.

Going Through – causing oneself or some material to go through a boundary and emerge at the other side.

Layering – placing materials in a layer, combining envelopment and on top schemas.

SUPPORTING HER SCHEMA AT NURSERY
When we plan for children's learning we use a chart called a PLOD (Possible Lines of Direction).

The purpose of the PLOD is to ensure staff provide children with a broad, wide and deep curriculum. Other children benefit from this type of planning. Chris Athey (1990, p. 30) points out,

'Unreflective child centredness has led to the false belief that every child requires a unique educational programme. Constructivist teachers know that many children share similar cognitive concerns.'

Becky's PLOD (Figure 8.6) relates to her interest in making parcels and envelopes. When we have planned effectively for the children's learning in this way then they are able to play and learn at a deep level. Becky is almost always engrossed when making parcels and presents. The planning matches her educational needs.

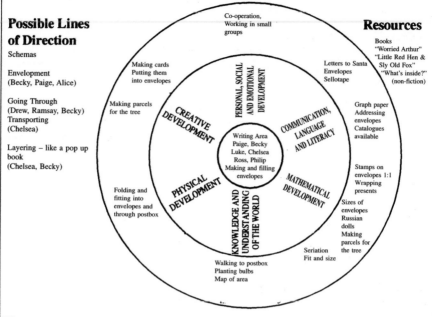

Figure 8.6 Becky's PLOD chart

SUPPORTING HER SCHEMA AT HOME

At home it is nearly Christmas time. Becky's envelopment schema has led her to make up lots of parcels. She enjoys cooking with mum, but is only interested in covering the cake with butter icing and chocolate buttons.

Becky received a pram for Christmas but rather than use it in the traditional manner she was more interested in filling it up and covering it up with a blanket.

Her Mum's Diary 4.1.98

'Becky's Christmas present from nursery was very successful. Four rolls of sellotape and a big roll of paper. She then proceeded to cut out all her Xmas cards and wrap each one into a parcel. 27 in total!'

13.3.98

'No nursery today – I gave her a roll of brown paper and some Sellotape and left her to it – by bedtime there was a huge pile of parcels for Alice, William and Sheree.'

THE EARLY LEARNING GOALS AND BEYOND

Physical Development – Becky is using her senses and physical actions. When Becky began wrapping parcels, it was all on a sensory motor level. She enjoyed the experience of playing with paper and sellotape while learning and developing new skills.

Communication, Language and Literacy – Becky's parcel making became more intricate. She began to work at a symbolic representation level. Her parcels and presents became gifts and messages for different people. She wrote the names of her family and friends on each parcel, using upper and lower case letters appropriately. Becky is developing her emergent writing.

Knowledge and Understanding of the World – Initially, Becky was making simple transformations by screwing up paper to make a parcel. She is now able to make complex transformations – she plans angles, makes corners, estimates size and fit, position and co-ordinates different surfaces.

Mathematics – Bending the paper when wrapping parcels involves spatial concepts and estimating how much paper is needed.

Personal Social and Emotional Development – Becky is thinking of others, and communicating with them.

Creative Development – She is making something of her own, for each of her special friends.

PROVISION FOR AN ENVELOPER

How do we support, extend and challenge Becky's thinking in nursery?

- We ensure that there is enough choice of provision, e.g. Sellotape, paper, string, hole punch, stickers etc.
- We encourage her to make her own decisions about what to use.
- We are interested in and supportive of what Becky is doing and try to extend her interests.
- We allow Becky to wallow in the experience and give her plenty of time to organise her thinking and carry out her ideas.
- We try to protect her space, so that she can use the provision optimally.

The school is not isolated from society but an integral part of it. The school has both the right and the duty to make this culture of childhood visible to the society as a whole, in order to provoke exchange and discussion. Sharing documentation is a true act of democratic participation.

(Rinaldi, 1998, p. 122)

Increasingly the documentation we produce at Pen Green contributes to the wider debate between parents, early years educators, politicians and policy-makers about critical issues in early childhood education.

Bibliography

Abbott, D. (1998) *Culture and Identity*, Hodder & Stoughton, London.

Allman, P. (1983) *The Nature and Process of Adult Development*, Open University Press, Buckingham.

Anderson, K. in Armitage, S., Jack, D. and Wittner, J. (1987) Beginning where we Are, *Oral History Review*, Vol. 15, pp. 103–27.

Arnold, C. (1967) Prejudice – racial, religious and class, unpublished study, Kirkby Fields Training College.

Arnold, C. (1990) *Children Who Play Together Have Similar Schemas*, Pen Green Centre, Corby.

Arnold, C. (1997a), Understanding young children and their contexts for learning and development: building on early experience. Unpublished MEd thesis, Leicester University.

Arnold, C. (1997b). Sharing ideas with parents about how children learn, in M. Whalley (ed.) *Working With Parents*, Hodder & Stoughton, London.

Arnold, C. (1999) *Child Development and Learning 2–5 Years, Georgia's Story*, Hodder & Stoughton, London.

Athey, C. (1990) *Extending Thought in Young Children: A Parent-Teacher Partnership*, Paul Chapman, London.

Atmore, E. (1999). Meeting the needs of young children through early childhood development policy. Warwick Conference.

Audit Commission (1994) *Seen but Not Heard: Developing Community Health and Social Services for Children in Need*, HMSO, London.

Ball, C. (1994) *Start Right: The Importance of Early Learning*, RSA, London.

Barber, M. (1996). *The Learning Game*, Victor Gollancz, London.

Bartholomew, L. and Bruce, T. (1993) *Getting to Know You*, Hodder & Stoughton, London.

Bertram, A. D. (1995) Adult engagement styles and their use in staff development. Paper presented at the 5th European Early Childhood Educational Research Association Conference, Sorbonne, Paris.

Bertram, A. D. (1996) Effective early childhood educators. Unpublished PhD thesis, Coventry University.

Bertram, A. D. Laevers, F. and Pascal, C. (1996) Grasping the quality of adult-child interactions in early childhood education settings: the adult style observation schedule, in S. Rayna, F. Laevers and M. Deleau (eds) *What are the Educational Objectives for Pre-School Education?* EECERA, INRP, Nathan, Paris.

Bertram, T. and Pascal, C. (2000) *Early Excellence Centres: First Findings Autumn 1999*, DfEE, London.

Bettelheim, B. (1990) *Recollections and Reflections*, Thames & Hudson, London.

Blakemore, C. (1998) Unpublished Paper at Pen Green Centre Conference on Giving Children a Sure Start, November, Corby.

Bredekamp, S. and Shephard, L. (1989) How best to protect children from inappropriate school expectations, practices and policies, *Young Children*, Vol. 44, no. 3, pp. 14–34.

Bright, J. (1998) Provision for young children, Implementation paper for the Cross-Departmental Review of Provision for Young Children, 26 February.

Bruce, T. (1997) *Early Childhood Education*, 2nd edn, Hodder & Stoughton, London.

Bruce, T. (1999) Seminar on pedagogic architecture. Unpublished paper presented at Pen Green in October.

Bruner, J. (1977) *The Process of Education*, 2nd edn, Harvard University Press, Cambridge, MA.

Burk-Rodgers, D. B. 91998) Supporting autonomy in young children, *Young Children*, May, pp. 75–80.

Ceppi, G. and Zini, M. (1998) *Children, Spaces, Relations, Meta Project for an Environment for Young Children. Reggio Children*, Somus Academy Research Centre, Milan.

Chandler, T. (1997) Daring to care – men and childcare, in M. Whalley (ed.) *Working with Parents*, Hodder & Stoughton, London.

Dahlberg, G. (1998) Seminar held at the Thomas Coram Foundation, London. Unpublished.

Dahlberg, G., Moss, P. and Pence, A. (1999) *Beyond Quality in Early Childhood Education and Care*, Falmer Press, London.

David, T. (ed.) (1994) *Working Together for Young Children*, Routledge, London.

Department of Health (1991) *The Children Act 1989: Guidance and*

Regulations, 2, Family Support, Daycare and Educational Provision for Young Children, HMSO, London.

DfEE (1996) *Early Excellence – a Head Start for Every Child*, Labour Party, London.

DfEE (1997) *Excellence in Schools*, DfEE in 3681, HMSO, London.

DfEE (1998) *Meeting the Childcare Challenge*, HMSO, London.

DfEE (1999a) *Sure Start: A Guide for Trailblazers*, DfEE, London.

DfEE (1999b) *Early Excellence Centres. First Findings, Autumn 1999*, DfEE, London.

Drummond, M. J. (1989) Early years education: contemporary challenges in early childhood education, C. W. Desforges (ed.) *British Journal of Educational Psychology*, Monograph Series No. 4.

Drummond, M. J. (1993) *Assessing Children's Learning*, David Fulton, London.

Dryden, G. and Vos, J. (1994) *The Learning Revolution*, Accelerated Learning, Aylesbury, Bucks.

Easen, P., Kendall, P. and Shaw, J. (1992) Parents and educators: dialogue and developing through partnership, *Children and Society*, Vol. 6, no. 4, pp. 282–96.

Edwards, C., Gandini, L. and Forman, G. (1998). *The Hundred Languages of Children: The Reggio Emilia Approach – Advanced Reflections*, 2nd edn, Ablex, London.

Epstein, D., Elwood, J., Hey, V. and Maw, J. (1998) *Failing Boys*, Open University Press, Buckingham.

Epstein, J. L., Elwood, J., Hey, V. and Maw, J. (1996) *Partnership 2000 Schools Manual*, Johns Hopkins University, Baltimore, MD.

Faulkner, D. (1995) Play, self and the social world, in P. Barnes (ed.) *Personal, Social and Emotional Development of Children*, Open University Press, Milton Keynes.

Fletcher, C. (1999) Home and school myth: parents don't care, in R. O'Hagan (ed.) *Modern Eduational Myths*, Kogan Page, London.

Freire, P. (1970) *Pedagogy of the Oppressed*, Penguin, Harmondsworth.

Freire, P. (1996) *Letters to Christina*, Routledge, London.

Fuerst, J. S. and Fuerst, D. (1993) Chicago experience with an early childhood programme: the special case of the Child Parent Centre Program, *Educational Research*, Vol. 35, no. 3, pp. 237–53.

Gardner, H. (1983) *Frames of Mind*, Basic Books, New York.

Gardner, H. (1991) *The Unschooled Mind*, Fontana, London.

Ghedini, P., Chandler, T., Whalley, M. and Moss, P. (1995) *Fathers, Nurseries and Childcare*, European Commission Equal Opportunities Unit/Early Childcare Network.

Goldschmied, E. (1991) What to do with the under twos. Heuristic play. Infants learning, in D. Rouse (ed.) *Babies and Toddlers; Carers and Educators. Quality for Under 3's*, National Children's Bureau, London.

Goleman, D. (1996) *Emotional Intelligence*, Bloomsbury, London.

Greenfield, S. (1997) *The Human Brain: A Guided Tour*, Weidenfeld & Nicholson, London.

Haggerty, M. (1996). *Using Video to Work With Te Whaariki*, Wellington College of Education, New Zealand.

Handy, C. (1997) *The Empty Raincoat*, Arrow Books, Reading.

Hargreaves, D. H. (1996) Teaching as a research-based profession; possibilities and prospects. Teacher Training Agency Annual Lecture, April.

Harlen, W. (1982) Evaluation and assessment, in C. Richards (ed.) *New Directions in Primary Education*, Falmer Press, London.

Hendricks, A. and Meade, A. (1993). *Competent Children: Influences of Early Childhood Experiences*, New Zealand Council for Educational Research, Wellington.

Hobbs, R. (1998) Team building for staff at Pen Green Centre, internal training session.

Holman. (1987) Research from the underside, *British Journal Social Work*, Vol. 17, pp. 669–83.

Isaacs, S. (1936) *Intellectual Growth in Young Children*, Routledge & Kegan Paul, London (first published in 1930).

Jack, D. in Anderson, K., Armitage, S., Jack, D. and Wittner, J. (1987) Beginning where we are, *Oral History Review*, Vol. 15, pp. 103–27.

Jordan, B. and Henderson, A. (1995) Interaction analysis: foundations and practice, *Journal of the Learning Sciences*, Vol. 41, no. 1, pp. 39–103.

Laevers, F. (1993) Deep level learning: an exemplary application on the area of physical knowledge, *European Early Childhood Education Research Journal*, Vol. 1, no. 1, pp. 53–68.

Laevers, F. (1994a). *The Leuven Involvement Scale for Young Children*, LIS-YC Manual and videotape, Experiential Educational Series no. 1, Leuven, Belgium, Centre of Experiential Education.

Laevers, F. (1994b). The innovative project: experiential education 1976–1995, *Studia Pedagogica*, Vol. 16, pp. 159–72.

Laevers, F. (1995) Lecture at EEL, Worcester College of Higher Education, September.

Laevers, F. (1997) *A Process-Oriented Child Follow Up System for Young Children*, Centre for Experiential Education, Leuven.

Lazar, I. (1983) *As the Twig is Bent: Lasting Effects of Pre-School*

Programmes, The Consortium of Longitudinal Studies, Hillsdale, NJ.

Lee, V. and Das Gupta, P. 1995) *Children's Cognitive Language Development*, Open University Press, Milton Keynes.

Mairs, K. (1990) *A Schema Booklet for Parents*, Pen Green Centre, Corby.

Malaguzzi, L. (1993) For an eduation based on relationship, *Young Children*, Vol. 11, pp. 9–13.

Malcolm, A. (1993) Fathers' invovement with their children and outside work commitments. Unpublished study submitted as part of a Diploma in Post-Qualifying Studies.

Marshall, J. (1996). Revisioning organisations by developing female values, in J. Boot, J. Lawrence and J. Morris (eds) *Managing the Unknown by Creating New Futures*, McGraw-Hill, London.

Meade, A. (1995), *Thinking Children*, New Zealand Council for Educational Research, Wellington.

Mezirow, J. (1977) Perspective transformation, *Studies in Adult Education*, 9 October, pp. 153–64.

Miller, R. L. (2000) *Researching Life Stories and Family Histories*, Sage, London.

Moir, A. and Moir, B. (1999) *Why Men Don't Iron: The New Reality of Gender Differences*, HarperCollins, London.

Moss, P. (1992) Perspectives from Europe, in G. Pugh (ed.) *Contemporary Issues in the Early Years*, Paul Chapman Publishing in Association with the National Children's Bureau, London.

Mullins, L. (1989) *Management and Organisational Behaviour*, Pitman, London.

Nash, J. M. (1997) Fertile minds, *Time Magazine*, 3 February.

Nucci, L. and Smetana, J., G. (1996) Mothers' concepts of young children's areas of personal freedom, *Child Development*, Vol. 677, pp. 1870–86.

Organization for European Co-operation and Development (OECD) (1997) *Parents as Partners in Schools*, OECD, Paris.

Oliver, C., Smith, M. and Barker, S. (1998). Effectiveness of early interractions. Paper for the Cross-Departmental Review of Provision for Young Children.

Pascal, C. (1996) Lecture at Pen Green Centre. Unpublished.

Pascal, C. and Bertram, A. D. (1994) Defining and assessing quality in the education of children from 4–7 years, in F. Laevers (ed.) *Defining and Assessing the Quality in Early Childhood Education: Studia Paedagogica*, Leuven University Press, Leuven.

Pascal, C., Bertram, A. (1977) *Effective Early Learning*, Hodder & Stoughton, London.

Pascal, C. and Bertram, A. D. and Ramsden, F. (1994) *Effective Early Learning: The Quality Evaluation and Development Process*, Amber Publications, Worcester.

Pen Green Centre/DfEE (1999) Autumn term evaluation project: pedagogic architecture. Unpublished paper.

Pen Green Research Base Report (2000) *Parent led needs assessment.* Unpublished internal document.

Plowden Report (1967). *Central Advisory Council for Education, Children and their Primary Schools*, HMSO, London.

Pollard, A. (1996) *The Social World of Children's Learning*, Cassell, London.

Pugh, G., De'Ath, E. and Smith, C. (1994) *Confident Parents, Confident Children*, National Children's Bureau, London.

Rinaldi, C. (1998) Projected curriculum constructed through documentation – Progettazione: an interview with Lella Gandini, in C. Edwards, L. Gandini and G. Forman, *The Hundred Languages of Children: The Reggio Emilia Approach – Advanced Reflections*, Ablex, London.

Rogers, C. R. (1983) *Freedom to Learn for the 80s*, Merrill, London.

Rutter, M. and Rutter, M. (1992) *Developing Minds*, Penguin, Harmondsworth.

Scott, P. (1996) He has seen the future and it gets harder: profile of Charles Handy, *Times Educational Supplement*, 29 November, p. 4.

Shaw, J. (1991) An investigation of parents' conceptual development in the light of dialogue with a community teacher. Unpublished PhD thesis, University of Newcastle-upon-Tyne,

Smiley, P. A. and Dweck, C. (1994) Individual differences in achievment and goals among young children, *Child Development*, Vol. 65, pp. 1723–43.

Smith, T. (1990) Parents and pre-school education, in N. Entwistle (ed.) *Handbook of Educational Ideas and Practices*, Routledge, London.

Sood, N. (1999) International perspectives and policy on early childhood provision, Warwick Conference, April.

Stimson, J. (1995) *Worried Arthur*, Ladybird, Loughborough.

Strauss, A. and Corbin, J. (1990) *Basics of Qualitative Research*, Sage, London.

Sylva, K. (1994) A curriculum for early learning, in C. Ball, *RSA Start Right: The Importance of Early Learning*, RSA, London.

Sylva, K. (1999) Linking quality processes to children's developmental outcomes, Keynote Lecture, Warwick Conference, April.

TES (2000) Early years shops save money, *Times Educational Supplement*, 25 February, p. 11.

Vygotsky. L. (1978) *Mind in Society*, Harvard University Press, Cambridge, MA.

Weinberger, J. (1996) *Literacy Goes to School: – The Parents' Role in Young Children's Literacy Learning*, Paul Chapman, London.

Whalley, M. (1992) A question of choice. Unpublished MA thesis, Leicester University.

Whalley, M. (1994). *Learning to be Strong*, Hodder & Stoughton, London.

Whalley, M. (1996a). Unpublished Paper for EECERA Conference, Lisbon.

Whalley, M. (1996b) *Confident Parents, Confident Children: Group Leader Notes*, Open University Press, Milton Keynes.

Whalley, M. (ed.) (1997a) *Working with Parents*, Hodder & Stoughton, London.

Whalley, M. (1997b) Parents' involvement in their children's learning. Conference paper, November.

Whalley, M. (1998) *Basic Skills Magazine*, March/April.

Whalley, M. (1999a) Leadership in early years settings. Unpublished PhD thesis, University of Wolverhampton.

Whalley, M. (1999b) Unsettled times, *Nursery World*, 16 September, pp. 10–11.

Whalley, M. and Arnold, C. (1997a). Parental involvement in education. Paper for Teacher Training Agency.

Whalley, M. and Arnold, C. (1997) Effective Pedagogic Strategies, TTA Summary of Research Findings, Teacher Training Agency, London.

Whalley, E. and Whalley, P. (1996) Making schemas easy to understand. Briefing paper for a conference at Pen Green Research, Development and Training Base.

Whitaker, P. (1986) A humanistic approach to teacher in-service education, *Self and Society*, Vol. 4, no. 6, pp. 276–81.

Wittner, J. in Anderson, K., Armitage, S., Jack, D. and Wittner, J. (1987) Beginning where we are, *Oral History Review*, Vol. 15, 103–27.

Wolfendale, S. and Einzig, H. (1999) *Parenting Education and Support*, David Fulton, London.

Yanez, Y., L. (1999) Networking for children; empowering families for early education in rural and resourceless communities in Venezuela, Keynote Lecture, Warwick Conference, April.

Index